IDENTITY

IDeNTiTY aND You

WHAT iS IDENTiTY?

Identity means who you are. People use this word to talk about who they are as a person.

Identity is everything that makes you *you*, from what you look like to what you think and believe to what you like to do. Your identity is everything that makes you who you are.

Everyone has an identity.

No other person in the world has the exact same identity as you.

Your identity is made up of many different parts. Some parts of your identity are easy to see—like the way you dress and how your natural hair looks. Some parts are not—like what you believe and how you think and feel.

Together, all of the different parts of your identity make you who you are!

WHAT iS MY IDENTiTY?

Your identity comes from your family and your community. (Find out what this word means on page 4!)

Your identity also comes from the people and things you see every day, like the people in your school and the shows you watch on television.

Your identity comes from the way you understand who you are and what people see and believe about you.

There are two different types of identity that people usually mean when they use the word: personal identity and social identity.

> A COMMUNITY is a group of people living together in the same place. The place can be your neighborhood or your city or town.
>
> Community can also mean a group of people who share the same ideas and goals, who care about the same things.

WHAT IS PERSONAL IDENTITY?

Your personal identity comes from you, your family, your community, the experiences you have, and the places around you.

It includes your names, the foods you like, and the people you love. Your personal identity also includes your relationship with your family members and the people you care about. It is also what you are good at doing, what you want to get better at doing, and the things you call your favorites.

Your personal identity is all about you—the parts of your identity that makes you different from other people!

This is Ruby! She has some personal identities she would like to share with you!

Ruby is eight years old.

Ruby lives with her mom and her ate Gabriela. (Ate is pronounced ah-tey.) They live in an apartment, and her lola lives in a house in the same neighborhood.

Ruby likes to dance, and fall is her favorite season. Her favorite color is green, and she loves ice cream! At school, Ruby likes Reader's Workshop because she likes to read a lot.

Ruby has a pet turtle that she found when she was playing a game of hide and seek with her friends. (The turtle's name is

Raphael!) The turtle lives in a big tank in a corner of the bedroom she shares with her sister.

Together, all of these things make Ruby's personal identity!

Some of Ruby's friends have similar identities and some have different ones. (You will get to meet her friends soon!)

WHAT IS SOCIAL IDENTITY?

Your social identity comes from the parts of you that relate to other people in your community and around the world.

Your social identities fit into different categories that have been named, created, and defined by society.

Some social identity categories are race, ethnicity, gender, citizenship, and class.

SOCIETY is a group of people living together in a community. It can also mean people in the larger world community. In many societies, people work together to make sure that there is peace, safety, and JUSTICE. (See page 41.) Not all societies have the same goal for all of the people in the community.

RACE is what other people see when they look at your skin color and skin tone, hair texture, and other parts of the way we look.

ETHNICITY is the parts of your identity that come from the common place or share the cultural traditions of all of the people in your family who were born before you.

GENDER is the way many people in society believe that a person should behave based on whether they have male or female body parts. A lot of people think there are just two genders, female and male, but there are many, many more!

CITIZENSHIP is having membership to a country by law. A CITIZEN is a person who is allowed by law to be a member of a country.

CLASS is a group of people who have a similar amount of money and resources. Someone who is in an upper class has a lot of money, and they are rich and have power. Someone who is in a lower class does not have a lot of money and may not own property or have much power. (Find out what "power" means on page 47.)

RaCe aND ETHNiCiTY

WHAT iS RACE?

Race is a part of your identity that does not usually change. It comes from the skin, hair, and other parts of the way we look that we were born with. Race will be a part of us throughout our whole lives.

When people talk about race, they are talking about what other people see when they look at your skin color and skin tone, hair texture, and other parts of the way you look.

People who look similar in these ways are part of the same group, even if they are not part of the same family. That group is called a race.

Everyone has a **racial identity**.

WHAT iS A RACiAL iDENTiTY?

Your racial identity comes from the race (or races) that you are a part of.

In the United States, the bigger groups for race that the government often uses are Black, American Indian or Alaska Native, Asian, Native Hawaiian and Pacific Islander, Latino/a/x/e and Hispanic, and white. These are the groups that people usually think of when talking about race. (Find out what these words mean on page 13!)

Some people may have racial identities that do not belong to any of these big groups. Some people may belong to more than one group!

Everyone has a racial identity.

This is Ruby's friend Shawn! His racial identity is Black.

Ruby's racial identity is biracial. Biracial means that her parents or ancestors have different racial identities. Ruby's mom is Asian American. Ruby's dad is Black.

WHY DO DIFFERENT PEOPLE HAVE DIFFERENT SKIN COLORS?

Everyone has skin. It protects everything in your body (your bones, your blood, your muscles, and your organs)!

Your skin has melanin. Melanin is the natural coloring of your skin. It helps to protect your skin from the sun.

Some people have more melanin than others. People whose ancestors are from places where the sunshine is more intense have darker skin. People whose ancestors are from places where there is less sunshine have lighter skin.

Your ANCESTORS are your family members who were born before you, including your grandparents, their grandparents, and so on. Some people know who their ancestors are. Some people do not know who their ancestors are.

The words you may use to describe skin color are not very clear. There are very few people who have skin that is as white as paper or as black as ink.

Everyone's skin has color, and that color comes in lots of different shades and tones!

Some of the words you can use to describe skin color are:

EBONY

GOLDEN BROWN

BEIGE

TAN

FRECKLED LIGHT PINK

DARK BROWN

There are so many different ways to describe the color of your skin! What words can you use to describe your skin color?

When people talk about being Black or Brown or white, they are not just talking about skin color. They are also talking about the community they have with all the people in the world who have skin like theirs, and the things they have in common!

For a long time in the United States, INDIGENOUS, Black and African, Asian, and Latine people have been called MINORITIES. (Find out what "indigenous" means on page 10!)

MINORITY means less than half, or a few. The number of Indigenous, Black, Asian, and Latine people in the world is a really big one.

There are more Black and Brown people in the world than there are white people.

PERSON OF THE GLOBAL MAJORITY is a term people use instead of using "minority." It is a more positive way to talk about Black and Brown people. It also helps everyone to remember that the group of People of the Global Majority around the world is a big one!

WHERE DID RACE COME FROM?

The idea of race has not always been around.

Race is a social construction. This is a big way to say that race was created by people in society.

A group of people who share the same racial identity are a racial group. The different racial groups we talk about today were made up by people in Europe hundreds of years ago.

It all started during a time when people from the continent of Europe, called Europeans, started to colonize countries all around the world. (Find out what "colonize" means on page 11.)

The people from Europe who were colonizers forced people out of their homes and communities and took control of everything. (Find out what "colonizers" means on page 11.)

In Central America and South America, the colonizers took freedom away from the indigenous people and forced them to work for the European people without pay. Enslaved people were treated very badly. They were scared, upset, angry, and unhappy.

INDIGENOUS PEOPLE means the first people. The people who were the very first to live on the land and in a particular place are INDIGENOUS. Sometimes, depending on where you live, indigenous people are called First Nations people, Native Americans, or Aboriginal people.

The European colonizers did this to people from Africa too. They took people of all ages from their homes in Africa and brought them to America without their permission. The colonizers forced these people to do hard work they did not want to do themselves.

These African people did not choose to come here. They did not choose to be enslaved.

An ENSLAVED PERSON is someone who does not have the freedom to live their life the way they want to live it. Part of their society says they are owned by another person, and they are made to work for free.

Some Europeans came to this country and worked as INDENTURED SERVANTS. They were not considered to be enslaved people.

What is the difference between an indentured servant and an enslaved person?

An indentured servant had the freedom to live their life the way they wanted to live it.

The indentured servant and the person they worked for had an agreement. After the servant had worked for several years, they were free to do whatever they wanted to do.

An indentured servant did not always choose to enter into that agreement. Sometimes they were made to become indentured servants as a result of the law or as a punishment.

An enslaved person did not have the freedom to live their life the way they wanted to live it. An enslaved person was never free.

The people who forced enslaved people to work did not see them as human beings. The people in charge thought of enslaved people as property. Property is anything that belongs to you-your books, your toys, and your clothes are your property. People are not property!

Enslaved people and their families-even children just like you-had to work for the people in charge for their whole lives.

COLONIZATION is when one group takes control of another group by force. (Most of the time, the first group will COLONIZE, by using violence to take control of the second group.) COLONIZERS are the people who take control.

The way that the Europeans forced enslaved people to do hard work for them without pay was called slavery.

Some people thought that slavery was a bad thing to do to other people. The Europeans who wanted to keep slavery needed to find ways to make it seem okay to the people who did not like it. To do this, they created ideas and beliefs that they used to convince these people (and themselves) that the bad things they were doing were actually good things.

These Europeans decided to use the fact that people look different to convince people that slavery was okay. They said that people with lighter skin were smarter, more beautiful, and better than people with darker skin. (This is not true!)

They did everything they could to find differences between people with lighter skin and people with darker skin, like measuring the size of people's heads, looking at people's brains after they died, and examining people from the inside and out.

One of the people who created the different racial groups that we use today was a scientist named Carl Linnaeus, from Sweden.

He wrote a book called *Systema Naturae* in the year 1735. That means he wrote the book more than two hundred years ago!

In that book, he shared his way to organize the world. He did this by putting things into different groups, like he did with plants, animals, and people. The groups he made up for people were based on where they lived and the color of their skin. The racial groups he created are still used today.

When Carl Linnaeus organized the world, he put plants, animals, and people into different groups. The groups were based on the way these living things looked, like the shape of the leaves on plants and skin color and facial features on people.

WHAT IS ETHNICITY?

Like race, ethnicity is a part of your identity that does not usually change. It comes from your family. Ethnicity will be a part of you throughout your whole life.

When people talk about ethnicity, they are talking about where all of the people in your family who were born before you came from.

People who are from a common place or who share cultural traditions may belong to the same social group. That group is called an ethnicity

Race and ethnicity are not the same, but sometimes people will talk about them like they are. Everyone has an *ethnic identity*.

WHAT IS AN ETHNIC IDENTITY?

Your ethnic identity comes from the **culture** that your ancestors shared with you and your family.

Your culture comes from the traditions and holidays you, your family, and your community celebrate together.

Your culture also comes from what you and your family believe and the languages you speak, read, or write together.

The things you eat, the clothing you wear, the games and sports you play, and how you play them are all a part of your culture!

Everyone has a culture. Everyone has an ethnic identity.

This is Ruby and Shawn's friend Dani! Their ethnic identity is Táino and Seminole. Their ancestors are from what is now called Puerto Rico and what is now called the United States.

Ruby's *ethnic identity* is Filipino and **African American**. Ruby's **ancestors** are from the continent of Africa (she doesn't know which countries) and the country Philippines.

DID YOU KNOW?

Did you know that the race groups that are often used by the government are not always based on the color of your skin, hair texture, and facial features? The different categories are a mix of race and ethnicity. Currently, the United States government uses the following categories around race:

The race group of Black or African American includes people who have ancestors who are from Africa. This group includes people who may be Egyptian, Ethiopian, Haitian, Jamaican, Nigerian, Somali, and so many more.

The race group of white includes people who have ancestors who are from Europe, Asia, and Africa. This group includes people who may be Egyptian, English, German, Irish, Italian, Lebanese, Spanish, and so many more.

The race group of American Indian or Alaska Native includes people who have ancestors who are indigenous to the country that is now called the United States. This includes what is now called Alaska. This group includes many, many different groups and people who may be from the Blackfeet Tribe, Diné, Haudenosaunee, from the Nome Eskimo Community, and so many more.

The race group of Asian American includes people who have ancestors who are from the continent of Asia. This group includes people who may be Burmese, Cambodian, Chinese, Filipino, Hmong, Indian, Indonesian, Japanese, Korean, Pakistani, Vietnamese, and so many more.

The race group of Native Hawaiian and Pacific Islander includes people who have ancestors who are indigenous to Hawaii, Samoa, Guam, and islands located in the Pacific Ocean. This group includes people who may be Chamorro, Fijian, Marshallese, Native Hawaiian, Tongan, Samoan, and so many more.

The race groups that are used by the government are not always the same. They have not always been what they are today and they will probably change when you are older. The groups have changed a lot over the past 700+ years! Different groups have been taken out or added, and the definitions of who is Black, who is Asian, who is white, and so on keep changing.

And did you know that Latino/a/x/e and Hispanic are not race groups? They are a part of ethnic identity. Latino/a/x/e includes people who are born in or have ancestors from Latin American countries. This group includes people who are from Brazil, Colombia, Cuba, the Dominican Republic, and so many more. Hispanic includes people who are from countries where Spanish is the language that most people speak. This group includes people who are from Argentina, the Dominican Republic, México, and so many more.

IDeNTiTY iN the UNiTeD STaTeS

WHO DECIDES WHAT MY IDENTiTIES ARE?

You decide what your personal identities are! (Your family and community may help you too.)

Your social identity is different. It is your identity that comes from other people in society who are in the same categories as you are. People do not get to choose which social categories they are in.

The different groups for social identities were created over many years. Sometimes the rules about who belongs in which group are very clear, and other times they can be very confusing.

If you were born in the United States, you are in the group of United States citizens.

If the first language you learned is Spanish or Tagalog, Arabic, Diné, or Keresan, or any language that is not English, you are in the group of non-native English speakers.

If the doctor said that you were a specific gender when you were born, but they got it wrong, you are in the group of transgender people.

People's understanding of the many different identity groups has grown and changed since the beginning of human history. Some of the categories and groupings have changed a lot and some have not over hundreds of years.

You may not always feel like your social identities fit who you really are. That is because they do not always fit!

Many of the social identity groups here were created by people like the Europeans. They made up different reasons why Black, Indigenous, and Brown people should be treated differently.

The people from Europe had power, and they wanted to keep it. Creating different social identity groups helped them to separate people. It also helped to make it seem like some people having more power than other people was a good thing.

Knowing where your social identities come from can help you to change them and to make them fit who you really are!

Ruby uses she/her/hers **pronouns**, and her *gender identity* is **cisgender** female. Cisgender (or cis) means that the way Ruby understands her gender is the same as the gender the doctor said she was when she was born.

Her **citizenship identity** is American and Philippine. Ruby has what is called dual citizenship. Ruby was born in the United States, so she is a citizen of this country. Her mom was born in the Philippines, and both Ruby and her ate have Philippine citizenship too.

Ruby and her family live in a rented apartment. Her mom works full-time at the grocery store, and they do not always have enough money for all the things they need and want. Their **class identity** is working class, because her mom makes enough money to pay the rent and have food, but they cannot buy extra things whenever they want them.

Your GENDER IDENTITY is the way you understand your gender and how that understanding is similar to or different from the gender the doctor said you were when you were born.

Your CITIZENSHIP IDENTITY is the country where you are a citizen.

Your CLASS IDENTITY is the group of people who have a similar amount of money and resources to the amount that you have.

ARE SOME IDENTITIES BETTER THAN OTHERS?

Many people in society believe that some identities are more important than other identities. They are wrong! The truth is that no identity is better than any other identity.

We are used to seeing the same type of people on television, in movies, in magazines, on the news, in our government, and in books.

Because we see this all the time, we start to believe that one type of person is "normal"—and that anyone else is "different."

Some people may believe that they are more important than others because their identities are the ones that we see all the time.

These people believe what the European colonizers wanted everyone to believe: that some identities are more beautiful, smarter, and more "normal" than other identities.

These people may be louder and may take up more space. They may make other people who are not like them feel like they need to be quiet or change what they look like or how they act.

This is not okay.

No one is better than anyone else!

WHAT IS THE DOMINANT CULTURE OF THE UNITED STATES?

The people we usually see most in movies, in the government, in books, and on television are usually white, cisgender people who are not too young and not too old.

They usually have money, nice clothes, and nice things. They also celebrate Christian holidays like Christmas and Easter. They usually live in cities or the suburbs and have jobs.

The families we usually see have a mom, a dad, and two or three kids. The kids go to a school where most everyone looks like them, including their teachers.

We see people like this as "normal." Even though some of these things have changed during our history, this idea of what is "normal" has been the *dominant culture* in the United States ever since the Europeans started colonizing the country hundreds of years ago.

This culture that is all around us affects the way that all of us think and feel, what we do, and how we do it. It is the culture of our society, and it affects our rules, our laws, and just about everything in our lives.

DOMINANT means having power and being controlling. The DOMINANT CULTURE is one that is shared by the people who have the most power in a country. People who are in the dominant culture have a lot of power.

DOES EVERYONE FIT INTO THE DOMINANT CULTURE?

You might fit into the dominant culture. You might not fit into the dominant culture.

Parts of your identity may be a part of the dominant culture. Parts of your identity may not be a part of the dominant culture.

Ruby does not totally fit into the dominant culture.

She is an eight-year-old Asian Black biracial kid who lives with just her mom and her ate.

She is different from the people we see as "normal" who are white, not too young and not too old, and have families with a mom, a dad, and two or three kids.

But there are parts of Ruby's identity that do fit into the dominant culture.

She is cis, and she is a United States citizen who speaks English, just like people we see as "normal."

Shawn does not totally fit into the dominant culture either.

He is an eight-year-old Black kid who lives with two moms.

Just like Ruby, he is different from the people we see as "normal" who are white, not too young and not too old, and have families with a mom, a dad, and two or three kids.

But there are parts of Shawn's identity that do fit into the dominant culture.

He is cisgender, and his family is Christian, just like people we see as "normal."

Dani does not fit into the dominant culture.

They are nine years old, and they are nonbinary, which means they do not identify only as either male or female. Dani uses they/them pronouns. They have golden brown skin, they are Indigenous and Puerto Rican, and they live with their grandparents as well as their parents and siblings.

Dani is different from the people we see as "normal" who are white, cis people who are not too young and not too old. They rarely see people like them in movies or books. Very few people who make laws and changes in the country are like them.

WHAT PARTS OF MY IDENTITY WILL ALWAYS BE THE SAME?

Some parts of your identity stay the same during your whole life.

Shawn's dark brown eyes and ebony skin will be the same throughout his life. His ethnic identity will not change either, and he will always be African American, Gambian, and Dominican.

WHAT PARTS OF ME AND MY IDENTITY CHANGE?

Some of your identities grow and change over time, just like you do.

Shawn's age and the things he likes will change. Right now, Shawn likes to swim and play with his dog.

How you understand your identities and who you are changes as you grow and learn more about yourself.

EVERY PART OF YOU IS THE BEST PART OF YOU!

The people who love you and care about you think so too!

You get to decide what the best parts of you are! No one else can do that for you.

You are exactly who you are meant to be!

WHo You ARe!

Sometimes when you need to remember that you are an amazing and awesome person, that you are a whole person, and that you are learning and growing, an *affirmation* can help!

An affirmation is a positive sentence, word, or phrase that can help you remember that you do not have to be anybody but yourself.

YOU CAN CREATE YOUR OWN AFFIRMATION OR USE ONE OF THESE:

SiMiLaR aND DiFFeReNT

WHAT MAKES PEOPLE SIMILAR TO EACH OTHER?

DiD YOU KNOW?

Did you know that humans are really similar to each other? People are 99.9% similar (that's almost 100%!). Your genetic makeup makes you much more similar to other people than you are different from them.

Your GENETIC MAKEUP is the genes that are passed down to you from your birth parents, their parents, and your **ancestors**.

Genes help to build your body. Genes tell your body what to do. They help to keep you healthy. Genes also decide what you will look like.

Your genetic makeup includes the genes that decide your eye color, your hair texture, whether you can curl your tongue or not, and so much more!

People from around the world need some of the same things in order to live. Everyone needs water, oxygen, and food. People need shelter for protection. The shelters and homes may look different, but they help to keep people safe from the weather (like the hot sun and freezing cold temperatures) and predators. People are all much more alike to one another than they are different.

THiNK ABOUT IT!

Think of all the people you know. Who are some of the people who are similar to you?

Who looks like you? Who likes the same things you do? How are you similar to people in your family, school, community, and around the world?

WHAT MAKES PEOPLE DIFFERENT FROM EACH OTHER?

Even though people are close to being 100% similar, there are many ways people are different! Your social identities and your personal identities help to make you different from other people.

The different social identity groups make people think they are more different too. These different groups can make people feel separate from people who are not in the same groups.

Here are some of the ways people are different from each other:

* PEOPLE LIVE IN DIFFERENT PARTS OF THE WORLD AND IN DIFFERENT TYPES OF HOMES.
* YOUR ANCESTORS COME FROM DIFFERENT PARTS OF THE WORLD.
* THE FOODS EVERYONE EATS ARE DIFFERENT BASED ON WHERE YOU ARE FROM.
* WHAT YOU LIKE TO DO, HOW YOU PLAY, AND WHO YOU PLAY WITH MAKE YOU DIFFERENT.
* THE TRADITIONS YOU AND YOUR FAMILY HAVE ARE DIFFERENT. WHAT YOU CELEBRATE AND HOW YOU CELEBRATE IS DIFFERENT.
* PEOPLE HAVE DIFFERENT CULTURES AND BELIEFS.

There are so many things that make people different.

THINK ABOUT IT!

Think of all the people you know. Who are some that are different from you?

Who does not look like you? Who likes different things than you do? How are you different from people in your community and around the world?

IS IT A GOOD THING OR A BAD THING THAT PEOPLE ARE DIFFERENT?

It is a good thing that people are different and we are not the same!

All the things that make people different, both big and small, help to make us who we are!

People solve problems and think differently. This means they can help each other out! Some people make art, write stories, or sing songs. People are creative in different ways. Some people really love math and solving equations. Some people love studying animals and their habitats. Some people love playing soccer and swimming.

Being different lets you share the things you love and are good at with others.

Ruby, Dani, and Shawn are all in the same classroom. They live in the same neighborhood too. They have known each other since they were in kindergarten.

Ruby, Dani, and Shawn all have different types of families:

Ruby lives with her mom, her ate, and her pet turtle named Raphael. Her lola lives nearby!

Shawn lives with his two moms and his dog.

Dani lives with their mom and dad, their grandparents, and their younger sibling.

Ruby, Dani, and Shawn all have different favorite colors:

Ruby likes the color green.   Dani likes the color purple.

Shawn likes the color yellow.

They think it is great that they all like different colors because when they are working on a school project together, they all reach for different-color markers.

Shawn, Dani, and Ruby like different subjects in school.

Shawn likes math.   Dani likes music.   Ruby likes reading.

Sometimes they help each other with different things in school, like classroom work or making friends.

Their differences help Ruby, Dani, and Shawn to be good friends!

TALKiNG ABoUT DiFFeReNCeſ

IS IT OKAY TO TALK ABOUT DIFFERENCES?

It is okay to talk about differences!

Talking about differences helps people to learn more about themselves and others.

Talking about differences is a good thing. If you do not talk about your differences, then you might start to believe in the stereotypes that you see and hear about people who are different from you.

A STEREOTYPE is a general idea or belief about a group of people that is not based on facts. Stereotypes make it seem like everyone of the same group is the same.

Stereotypes are usually not true.

An example of a stereotype is that only girls should play with dolls. The truth is anybody and everybody can play with dolls. It does not matter what your gender is. Dolls are toys that anyone can play with.

Talking about differences and sharing what is true can help to get rid of stereotypes.

Talking about differences can sometimes make people feel uncomfortable.

It can be hard for people to talk about all of the amazing differences we have because they have not talked about them before.

The dominant culture of the United States has been the culture of our country for a long time. People have believed the dominant culture to be the "normal" culture of our country for hundreds of years. There really is no such thing as a normal way to be.

Ruby, Dani, and Shawn's teacher helped them to share some of the ways they are similar and different. Each person in their classroom made an identity map. When they were done, Dani, Shawn, Ruby, and their classmates shared their maps! They talked about who they are. They learned about the ways they are similar to each other and the ways they are different from each other. They learned new things about each other!

AN IDENTITY MAP IS A MAP YOU MAKE ALL ABOUT WHO YOU ARE!

You can put your social identities and your personal identities on it.
You choose what you will share with others!

Ruby learned a new word: multiethnic. That means a person has many ethnic identities. Ruby learned that some of her other classmates are multiethnic too! She also learned she is the only kid who has a pet turtle.

Dani learned that some of the other kids in their classroom are nonbinary and use the pronouns they/them too! They also learned that a lot of their classmates like to build with LEGOs.

Shawn learned that there are other kids in his class who have ADHD too! He also learned that a lot of his classmates like chocolate chip cookies.

HOW CAN WE TALK ABOUT DIFFERENCES?

There are many ways to start talking about differences.

One of the best ways to start talking with people about differences is to listen.

You can listen to what people call themselves when you first meet each other.

You can listen to how people talk about themselves and which words they use.

You can listen and learn about what things they like to do.

You can listen to find out about who their families and friends are.

There really is so much to listen for!

What else can you listen for?

You can ask questions too! You will not always know how people identify. People do not always talk about their social identities or their personal identities. Questions will help you to learn even more about people!

You can ask questions like—

"How do you identify?"

"What would you like me to call you?"

"How do you describe your skin color?"

"Can you tell me about some of the things you like to do?"

What other questions can you ask?

Sometimes people may want a little help with sharing who they are. When that happens, you can begin by sharing a little bit about who you are.

When you first meet someone, you can share the name you like to use and the pronouns you use.

Hi! I'm Ruby. I use **SHE/HER** pronouns.

I'm Shawn. I use **HE/HIM** pronouns.

I am a **BLACK CIS BOY**.

I have a pug dog named **MALCOLM**.

How do you identify? Do you have any pets?

Sometimes it is hard to start talking about your identities. It can be hard talking about your differences. If you are comfortable, you can share a little bit about yourself! (It's your choice!) This will help the people you are talking with to share their differences too!

It is important that people listen to you too! You can tell people how you identify and the words you use to describe who you are.

You can learn a lot about other people from listening to them. Other people can learn a lot about you when they listen to you! You can tell them what you like to be called and share the pronouns you use. You can talk about how you identify.

Even if you are ready to share, not everyone will want to talk about who they are—and that's okay! When you share with other people, make sure that you leave time and space for others to decide if they are ready!

WHAT IF I SAY SOMETHING WRONG?

Talking about differences is not easy.

Sometimes you will say the wrong thing.

You will make mistakes. People make mistakes.

Sometimes you will say things that will hurt other people.

If you say something that makes someone feel upset and hurt, you can start to repair with them.

To repair with someone means that you will work to make things better. You take responsibility for how you hurt the other person.

When you repair with someone you start by admitting you said something wrong. You can say something like, "What I said was not okay."

You can apologize and let them know you are sorry for upsetting and hurting them. You can say something like, "I'm really sorry and I will not do this again, I know it upset you." (Make sure that you really do mean what you are saying when you apologize.)

If the person you hurt wants to talk to you, you will need to listen. They might also not be ready to talk to you, and that is okay.

The person you hurt might not be ready to accept your apology. That is okay.

People need time and space to start to feel better again.

YOU WILL NOT ALWAYS GET IT RIGHT.

YOU CAN WORK ON MAKING SURE YOU DO NOT SAY THE WRONG THING AGAIN.

YOU WILL GROW FROM YOUR MISTAKES.

YOU ARE ALWAYS LEARNING AND GROWING.

You might say someone's name incorrectly. If this happens, you can apologize for saying their name wrong. You can then learn how to say their name the right way. Practice saying their name to yourself and to a friend. Say their name the right way the next time you talk to them.

You might say something to someone that was based on a stereotype. This is not okay. You do not need to wait for someone to tell you that what you said was wrong. You can apologize and begin to repair right away!

You KNoW WHo You ARe!

You know who you are better than anyone else!

You are the one who gets to choose how you identify!

You get to decide how much you will share with others.

You know who you are.

You are learning more about yourself and your history every day.

No one else knows you as well as you know yourself!

No one else can tell you who you are.

It does not feel good when other people try to tell you who you are.

It can make you feel angry and sad. It might even make you question who you are and make you feel confused. This is not okay.

You have a right to be yourself.

You have a right to be protected, to be heard, to be seen, to be respected, and to be a part of your community and society.

You decide which words you will choose and how you will share your identity with other people. No one else gets to decide that for you!

PuTTiNG IT ALL ToGeTHeR

✳ Your identity is everything that makes you who you are. Every person has an identity!

✳ Your identity is made up of many different parts.

✳ There are two different types of identity that people usually mean when they use the word—personal identity and social identity.

✳ Your personal identity comes from you, your family, your community, the experiences you have, and the places around you.

✳ Your social identity comes from the parts of you that relate to other people in your community and around the world.

✳ When people talk about race, they are talking about what other people see when they look at your skin color and skin tone, hair texture, and other parts of the way you look.

✳ Everyone has a racial identity.

✳ Everyone's skin has color, and that color comes in lots of different shades and tones!

✳ Race is a social construction. This is a big way to say that race was created by people in society.

✳ The different races, or racial groups, were made up by people in Europe hundreds of years ago. It all started during a time when people from Europe, called Europeans, started to colonize countries all around the world.

✳ These Europeans decided to use the fact that people look different to convince people that slavery was okay.

✳ When people talk about ethnicity, they are talking about where all of the people in your family who were born before you came from.

✳ Everyone has an ethnic identity. Everyone has a culture.

✳ You decide what your personal identities are! (Your family and community may help you too.) Your social identity is different. It is your identity that comes from other people in society who are in the same categories as you are.

✳ No identity is better than any other identity!

✳ The dominant culture of the United States is the culture that is all around us. It affects the way that all of us think and feel, what we do, and how we do it. It is the culture of our society, and it affects our rules, our laws, and just about everything in our lives.

✳ You might fit into the dominant culture. You might not fit into the dominant culture. Parts of your identity may be a part of the dominant culture. Parts of your identity may not be part of the dominant culture.

✳ Some parts of your identity stay the same during your whole life.

✳ Some of your identities grow and change over time, just like you do!

✳ You are exactly who you are meant to be!

✳ People are much more similar to one another than they are different!

✳ The different social identity groups make people think they are more different than they really are. The different social identity groups can make people feel separate from people who are not in the same groups.

✳ It is a good thing that people are different and we are not the same!

✳ Talking about differences helps people to learn more about themselves and others.

✳ A stereotype is a general idea or belief about a group of people that is not based on facts. Stereotypes make it seem like everyone of the same group is the same.

✳ One of the best ways to start talking with people about differences is to listen.

✳ If you say something that makes someone feel upset and hurt, you can start to repair with them.

✳ To repair with someone means that you will work to make things better. You take responsibility for how you hurt the other person.

✳ No one else knows you as well as you know yourself! No one else can tell you who you are.

JUSTICE

BiaS, PReJuDiCe, aND DiSCRiMiNaTioN

WHAT iS FAIRNESS?

Being *fair* means everyone gets what they need. Most of the time *fairness* means we are making sure things are equal and just for people. (Find out what "equal" means on the next page and what "just" means below.) Fairness is something people all understand differently because everyone is different.

Your *identities* and your experiences help you to understand what is fair and what is not.

WHAT iS JUSTiCE?

> Not everyone needs the same things to feel safe and cared for, because we are all different.

Being *just* means being fair. *Justice* is something that happens when people are treated fairly. It is when every person gets what they need to be healthy, cared for, and safe.

THiNK ABOUT IT!

There are 5 people. There are 15 cookies for them to share.

How can they share the cookies so it is most fair?

If each person gets 3 cookies each, is that fair?

What if one of the people has a whole box of cookies at home?

What if another person did not eat breakfast or lunch?

Is it still fair if each person gets 3 cookies each?

What could be fair?

How could each person get what they need?

IS EQUAL THE SAME THING AS FAIR?

Equal means having the same amount of something. It can also mean having the same rights and freedoms.

What is equal is not always what is fair.

Most of the time, equal means the same.

Equal is not always what is best and fair for everyone, because not everyone needs the same things.

> EQUITY is another word you might hear people use when talking about fairness and equality. Equity is when you get what you need, which may be different for different people because not everyone needs the same things.

THINK ABOUT IT!

Let's go back to the cookies!

It is not really fair if each person gets the same number of cookies when one person has a lot at home and another has not eaten anything.

It is more equitable if the person who has a bunch of cookies gives some of theirs to the person who has not eaten anything because what they need is not the same.

EQUITABLE means each person getting what they need.

WHAT IS BIAS?

A **bias** is a belief about a person, a group of people, a place, or a thing.

Everyone has biases.

Usually, your biases are hidden. You are not always aware of what biases you have.

Sometimes biases are good. Sometimes biases are not good.

Biases come from the things you see and hear. They come from your experiences and ideas. Biases are a way people try to understand the world around them. Where you are from, what you believe, and the people in your life help you to create biases. Sometimes your biases can be good and sometimes they are not.

STEREOTYPES also have a big effect on the way you think. Stereotypes you believe help to create your biases too.

Remember, a stereotype is a general idea or belief about a group of people that is not based on facts. Stereotypes make it seem like everyone of the same group is the same.

Stereotypes are usually not true.

You might believe a stereotype that all people who are tall are good at playing basketball. This is true for some people, but not all tall people are good at basketball or even like the sport.

Everybody has biases. You have biases. You might have a bias against another kid at school.

Your bias might come from having a bad time with someone who looks like the kid at school. Your bias might come from people in your family telling you not to play with kids like them. Your bias might come from something the kid said or did one time. Your bias might come from you not knowing anyone else like the kid at school.

Because of your bias against the kid at school, you might not play with them on the playground or you might get upset when the teacher asks you to work together.

When you have a bias against someone, that can make it hard for you to get to know the person. It can make you both feel bad, sad, hurt, and angry. Negative biases can lead to being unfair.

Biases can change.

Sometimes you are aware of your biases and sometimes you are not.

When you know what biases you have, you can work on changing them.

You can change your biases.

Everyone has biases.

Biases can change.

WHAT IS PREJUDICE?

Prejudice is a belief, attitude, or feeling about a person or group of people. Prejudice comes from not having all of the right information. They come from no real reasons or thoughts or experiences.

Everyone has prejudices.

Unlike your biases, usually you and other people are aware of your prejudices.

Most of the time prejudice can be bad.

Prejudices come from the world around you. They come from your family, friends, and the people in your life. Prejudice comes from your community and where you live. Prejudices come from what you see and hear, and what you believe. They also come from the stereotypes and biases you have.

Everyone has prejudices.

Most of the time prejudices are negative. Negative prejudices can lead to the unfair and hurtful treatment of people.

Everyone has prejudices.

Prejudices can change.

WHAT IS DISCRIMINATION?

Discrimination is the unfair, unequal, and unjust treatment of people. It is hurtful. Discrimination is not okay.

Unlike biases and prejudice, which are things you can believe and feel, discrimination is something you do. Discrimination is the way you act on your negative biases and prejudices.

Some ways a person may experience discrimination are:

- BEING EXCLUDED FROM PLAYING WITH OTHERS
- EXCLUDING OTHERS
- BEING TREATED UNFAIRLY
- TREATING OTHERS UNFAIRLY
- BEING CALLED NAMES

- CALLING OTHERS MEAN NAMES
- BEING BULLIED
- BULLYING OTHERS
- BEING HURT BY OTHERS
- HURTING OTHERS

Discrimination is not okay.

People discriminate. You might DISCRIMINATE against other people, or you might know someone who does.

A teacher might have a prejudice against kids who are from your neighborhood. They might not like the color of your skin or the kind of home you live in. The teacher might believe stereotypes that you and all the kids from your neighborhood are the same. Because of their prejudice, the teacher might discriminate against you. They might spend less time helping you. The teacher might be nicer to the kids from other neighborhoods and unkind to you. This is not okay. Discrimination is not okay.

WHAT ARE SOME EXAMPLES OF DISCRIMINATION?

Discrimination is the unfair and unjust treatment of people.

Discrimination is not okay.

Here are some examples of discrimination:

- **NOT BEING ALLOWED TO WEAR YOUR HAIR IN LOCS OR CERTAIN TYPES OF BRAIDS IS UNFAIR AND UNJUST**

- **BEING TOLD YOU HAVE TO USE A BATHROOM FOR THE GENDER YOU ARE NOT IS UNFAIR AND UNJUST**

- **BEING TOLD YOU CANNOT SPEAK YOUR HOME LANGUAGE AT SCHOOL IS UNFAIR AND UNJUST**

- **BEING EXCLUDED BECAUSE OF YOUR IDENTITIES IS UNFAIR AND UNJUST**

- **A TEACHER OR ADMINISTRATOR TREATING SOME OF YOUR CLASSMATES NICELY AND SOME UNKINDLY IS UNFAIR AND UNJUST**

- **BEING TOLD YOU ARE TROUBLE BECAUSE OF THE NEIGHBORHOOD YOU ARE FROM IS UNFAIR AND UNJUST**

- **BEING IGNORED BY YOUR TEACHER IS UNFAIR AND UNJUST**

Can you think of some other examples of discrimination?

Discrimination is not okay. It is unfair and unjust.

WHAT DOES UNJUST MEAN?

Unjust means something is not fair. Injustice is when something is unfair and unjust.

Justice is when everyone is treated fairly.

Injustice is when people are not treated fairly and when some people are treated as if they are not as important as others.

PoWeR

WHAT iS POWER?

Each person has **power**. Power is having control over yourself and having the freedom to make choices and change. This type of power is personal power.

People have power. When people get together to make change and work together, you have group power, or people power.

Institutions have power. They can make traditions, rules, and laws that affect people, communities, and society. This type of power is institutional power.

An INSTITUTION is an organized group of people or several different organized groups of people working together. Institutions have existed for a long time. The people or groups in an institution change, but the institution does not change much. Institutions help to make rules, laws, and traditions for people in society.

Everybody is affected by institutions.

Some of the different institutions that affect us are education, government, business, entertainment, health care, banking, and housing. (If you don't know what some of these words mean, talk with your friends or ask an adult!)

Here are some examples of smaller institutions: schools, hospitals, banks, prisons, businesses and stores, city or town halls, mosques, synagogues, churches, and other places of worship. For example, the entertainment institution includes smaller institutions like television stations, book publishers, musicians, and social media companies.

WHO HAS POWER?

YOU have POWER!

EVERYONE HAS POWER!

But not everyone is welcomed, encouraged, or asked to use their power.

People and institutions have power and can use their power to make positive change.

People and institutions can also use their power to have a negative effect.

WHY DO SOME PEOPLE HAVE MORE POWER THAN OTHERS?

Some people have more power than others in this country.

People who are members of the **dominant culture** of our country have A LOT of power.

Not everyone who is a member of the dominant culture chooses to have a lot of power or even wants to have a lot of power. They just have it. This is because our country is set up in a way that makes sure people who are a part of the dominant culture have more power. Institutions, rules, laws, and traditions help to make sure people in the dominant culture have a lot more power. (This has been happening for a long time!)

When people and institutions have a lot of power, they have more control over things. Some of the things they can control are money, resources, materials, and even people.

Sometimes when people have a lot of power it is called privilege, superiority, or advantage. Whatever it is called, it is still power!

Do you remember when you learned about the dominant culture on page 16?

In the United States, most everything is based off the dominant culture. The rules, laws, programs, and even the holidays celebrated are all based on the things that the dominant culture has believed in and allowed to continue for hundreds of years.

You will almost always see people who are members of the dominant culture as the people who are in charge and have power. Because of this, you may start to believe that people of the dominant culture are the ones who should hold all the power.

No one should have more power over anyone else because of the color of their skin or where their ancestors are from.

No one should have more power over anyone else because of their gender or who they love.

No one should have more power over anyone else because of their age or abilities.

No one should have more power over anyone else because of their religion or where they were born.

THINK ABOUT IT!

What do you notice when you look at all of the presidents of the United States?

They are all cis Christian men.

President Barack Obama is the only Black president our country has ever had! All of the other presidents are white.

Vice President Kamala Harris is the first Black, South Asian woman to be vice president in this country.

You may notice that there are more Black, Indigenous, People of the Global Majority, trans, and nonbinary people holding positions of power as you continue to grow. This can be a great thing!

WHAT iS OPPRESSION?

Oppression is a word used to describe when power is misused and abused and it happens on purpose.

Oppression is unfair and unjust. It has a negative effect on people and society.

Oppression is when one group of people believe they are better than another and discriminate and misuse their power against the others.

A person and groups of people can be oppressed.

A person, groups of people, and institutions can oppress people.

Personal power and institutional power can be misused and abused.

When people and communities are being oppressed, power is taken away.

Resources, land, language, **culture**, and identity are taken away.

Rules, laws, customs, and all types of violence are things that people and institutions use to oppress people.

Colonization is a form of oppression.

Colonization is when one group (usually people from the dominant culture) takes control of another by force (which is always violent).

When the **Europeans** came to the Americas, that was colonization.

Most countries in the world were colonized by a Western European country. But not all were. Some were colonized by non-Western European countries.

The land that is now called the United States was colonized by England.

The land that is now called Puerto Rico was first colonized by Spain and then by the United States.

The land that is now called Tanzania was colonized by Germany.

The land that is now called Brazil was colonized by Portugal.

The land that is now called the Philippines was first colonized by Spain and then by the United States (like Puerto Rico).

The land that is now called Ghana was colonized by England.

The land that is now called Vietnam was colonized by France.

That land that is now called Tibet was (and still is) colonized by China.

The land that is now called Taiwan was colonized by Japan.

The land that is now called Armenia was colonized by Russia.

Can you think of more countries that were colonized by other countries?

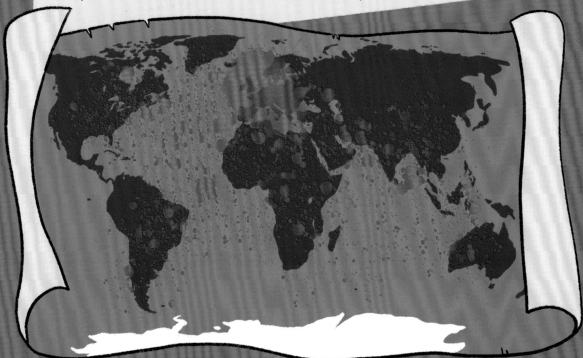

WHAT ARE SOME EXAMPLES OF OPPRESSION?

There are many different kinds of oppression. People who are oppressed usually have **social identities** that are not the same as the identities people in the dominant culture have.

> The dominant culture is hard to get away from. It is everywhere. Even though it is the culture that is dominant in our country, it is not what is best for everyone.

People can be oppressed because of their **race**, gender, size, religion, home country, who they love, and for any other way they may be different from the people who have the most power in our society.

Some of the different kinds of oppression are **ableism**, **ageism**, **cissexism**, **classism**, **heterosexism**, **racism**, and **sexism**.

There are other kinds of oppression too, but we will not learn about all of them in this book. Some of the other kinds of oppression are transphobia, antisemitism, islamophobia, homophobia, xenophobia, and religious oppression.

Ableism is discrimination and oppression against people who have visible or not visible physical, emotional, or **neurological** and mental disabilities. Ableism favors people who do not have disabilities. People with disabilities are oppressed.

NEUROLOGICAL means about nerves or the nervous system.

Ageism is discrimination and oppression against people who are 18 and younger (children) and elders. Children and teenagers have very little to no legal power in the United States. Ageism favors people who are adults, especially between the ages of 25 and 50. Children, teenagers, and elderly people are oppressed.

DiD YOU KNOW?

The United States is the only country in the world that has not accepted the United Nations Convention on the Rights of the Child (UNCRC). The UNCRC is a human rights agreement between almost all of the countries in the world. It states that all children have rights! Everyone who is 18 years and younger should have access to education, health care, and safety. Children should be able to grow in a place where they are cared for, loved, and understood.

LGBTQQIP2AA+ means people who are lesbian, gay, bisexual, transgender, questioning, queer, intersex, pansexual, two-spirit, androgynous, asexual, and more!

Heterosexism is discrimination and oppression against people based on who they love. It favors people who are or want to be in a relationship that is between only a woman and a man. This is often referred to as being "straight." People who are LGBTQQIP2AA+ are oppressed.

Cissexism is discrimination and oppression against people who are **transgender** or nonbinary, or people whose gender expression does not follow the common expectations of their gender. Cissexism favors people who are cis male or female. Trans, nonbinary, and gender nonconforming people and everyone who is not cis female or cis male are oppressed.

CISGENDER, or cis, means the way you understand your gender is the same as the gender the doctor said you were when you were born.

Classism is discrimination and oppression against people who do not have a lot of money or resources. It favors people who have a lot of money and resources. People who are living in poverty, people who are experiencing homelessness, and people who do not have a lot of resources and money are oppressed.

Racism is personal prejudice and bias and the planned misuse and abuse of power by institutions. It is discrimination and oppression against people based on the color of their skin, their hair texture, facial features, and where their ancestors came from. Racism favors people who are white and have ancestors from Europe. Black, Indigenous, Asian, and **Latine** People of the Global Majority are oppressed.

Sexism is discrimination and oppression against people who are not cis male. It favors cis men. Women, trans and nonbinary people, and people who are not cisgender male are oppressed.

INTERSECTIONALITY is a word used to help people understand that anyone can have more than just one identity at any one time. It also helps us to understand that some parts of a person's identity may give them power.

Everyone has an identity.

Everyone's identity has many different parts.

Your identity includes your race, gender, religion and what you believe, and so much more.

Intersectionality helps people to understand that all the different parts of your identity are not separate. It is important to look at a person as a whole person made of many different parts of their identity.

Everyone experiences identity differently.

Everyone's experiences are different because of identity.

Everyone has parts of their identities that come together.

When parts of a person's identity are oppressed, that person experiences the world differently than someone who is a part of the dominant culture.

Intersectionality helps us to see that even though people share some parts of their identity with each other, they are not the same.

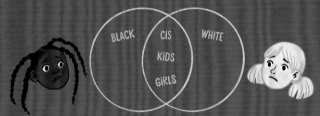

A Black cis girl and a white cis girl share that they are both cisgender. They both experience sexism because they are both cis girls. They both experience ageism because they are kids.

They do not share the same race. The white girl's race gives her more power and privilege. The Black girl's race does not give her power or privilege.

People hold more prejudice and bias against the Black girl. There are different rules and laws in different states that are unfairly unjust to her and other Black people. (You can learn more about some of these rules and laws in some of the books listed at the end of this book.)

The Black girl will experience more discrimination, prejudice, and oppression throughout her life than the white girl because of her RACIAL IDENTITY.

RACISM

WHAT IS RACISM?

RACISM is PERSONAL PREJUDICE and BIAS and the PLANNED MISUSE and ABUSE of POWER by INSTITUTIONS.

Racism is the unfair and unjust treatment of People of the Global Majority based on the idea that white people are better.

Racism is prejudice and discrimination against people based on their race (and ethnic identity).

Racism is the oppression of People of the Global Majority based on the idea that they should have less privilege, power, and resources than white people.

WHO INVENTED RACISM?

No one person invented racism. Racism has been around for hundreds and hundreds of years.

Do you remember when some people from Europe started to colonize countries all over the world? They forced people out of their homes and communities and took control of everything.

The COLONIZERS used the fact that people look different to convince people that colonization and enslavement was okay. Do you remember how they came up with reasons why some people should be enslaved and others should not?

There is not one clear day when racism began. We think racism started in the 1400s.

It became even more accepted in the 1600s and 1700s.

Scientists and some church institutions in parts of Europe helped to make a SOCIAL RANKING that put people in society into different groups based on the color of their skin, their facial features, and where they and their ancestors were from. (Turn the page!)

A SOCIAL RANKING is a way to put people into different groups. Some people were put into the top group and some people were put into the bottom group. The social ranking that was made put white Europeans at the very top and Indigenous and Black people at the bottom. The people who were at the top of the social ranking were believed to be more important than the people who were put into the bottom. Europeans worked hard to make sure this social ranking became the normal way of thinking.

The people from Europe and people in the dominant culture needed to get themselves and other people to believe that colonization and enslavement was okay. The social ranking was created by some people from Europe because they wanted to believe that oppressing people in other countries was okay. They wanted to believe that oppressing people who have darker skin was okay.

People from Europe who had power and money used the social ranking that was made by scientists to get people to believe that white Europeans were better than everyone else. They wanted to believe that white Europeans were smarter, more beautiful, and should have the most power. They also believed Indigenous and Black People of the Global Majority were not as smart or good enough and that they were less than human. The European people who believed in the social ranking believed that colonization and enslavement were good things for Black and Brown people. (Really, they were not!)

Colonization and enslavement were not good things.

The beliefs the people from Europe made up are not true. They are unfair and unjust.

The people from Europe were not any smarter, more beautiful, or worthy of power than any People of the Global Majority.

African, Asian, and Indigenous people had amazing empires long before the people in Europe ever did. Colonization and enslavement took all of that away.

Racism was created by white people from Europe and was used to make Black and Brown people seem like they were less human.

The different groups in the social ranking and racism helped the European people and people in the dominant culture to make sure power stayed with the people in the dominant culture (white, cis men).

Racism has been around for hundreds of years, and it is still here today. The more we know about racism, the better we can change the way we do things and work to dismantle it!

DISMANTLE means to take something apart, break it, and knock it down. To dismantle racism means we will work hard to make sure it does not keep happening. We will knock down and break racism!

HOW DO INSTITUTIONS HELP RACISM GROW?

Institutions help racism grow. They help to make sure that the dominant culture is everywhere in the United States.

Television, movies, magazines, books, and social media are all a part of the entertainment and media institution.

People in the dominant culture are always in movies, on television, and in books and magazines a lot more than People of the Global Majority. Because we see white, cisgender people so much more, we begin to think that is the only way to be normal. There is no one way to be normal. We also often see People of the Global Majority shown in ways that are harmful and create and keep stereotypes going. Because we see these stereotypes so often, people start to believe them to be true. This is not okay.

Schools are a part of the education institution.

The history of Indigenous, Black, and Brown people is not taught in schools as much as the history of people in the dominant culture. Instead, you talk more about people from Europe who colonized the country you live in. If you do learn about People of the Global Majority, it is usually only for a little bit of time. You might only learn about the bad things that happened to Black and Brown people. The stories are about hurt and pain and not about joy and the great things we have done. Because we mostly learn about the people in the dominant culture, we begin to think that the history of People of the Global Majority does not exist or that it does not matter. The history of Indigenous, Black, and Brown People of the Global Majority does matter.

People who work in schools are a part of the education institution too.

All people have biases and prejudices. Some biases and prejudices are negative. Some teachers believe Black students are not as good as other students. Black students are much more likely to be sent out of the classroom than white students. (This happens when they do not do anything wrong too.) Black students are much more likely to get detention or to be suspended from school because many teachers have a bias against Black students. This is not okay.

When institutions make rules and laws that are unfair and unjust for Indigenous, Black, and Brown People of the Global Majority, they are helping to keep racism going and helping it to grow.

DID YOU KNOW?

In 1790 the NATIONALITY ACT became a law that defined who could be a CITIZEN of the United States and who could not. People who were free, white men who owned property and had lived in the country for two years could get CITIZENSHIP. People who were not able to become UNITED STATES CITIZENS were Native Americans, Asian IMMIGRANTS, free Black people, Mexican immigrants, women, INDENTURED SERVANTS, ENSLAVED PEOPLE, and, really, anyone who was not a man from Western Europe. An immigrant is a person who moves to a new country. A lot of people were not able to become citizens of the United States, which meant they did not have the same rights as citizens. They could not vote, and buying property and owning businesses were more difficult for non-citizens. The Nationality Act was the first of many laws over 150 years that were created to keep Black and Brown People of the Global Majority from having equal rights. The Nationality Act was unfair and unjust. The government misused and abused its power to exclude a lot of people from being able to become citizens.

The United States government forced more than 100,000 Indigenous people living in the states that are now called Georgia, Florida, Alabama, North Carolina, and Tennessee to leave their homes and land. The INDIAN REMOVAL ACT of 1830 gave President Andrew Jackson the power to remove Native Americans from their homes and force them to walk hundreds of miles west to what was called "Indian territory." White settlers wanted the land of the Native Americans to grow cotton and other crops that they could trade and make money with. The Indian Removal Act was unfair and unjust. The government misused and abused their power by forcing people from the land they lived on and making them walk far away to new territory that was difficult to farm. About 4,000 Indigenous people died on the forced march, which is also known as the "Trail of Tears."

In the 1850s, people from China were the largest group of immigrants from Asia. Many of the immigrants who came worked as laborers and helped construct cities along the west coast of the country and build the TRANSCONTINENTAL RAILROAD. The transcontinental railroad connected different parts of the United States together and made trade and travel much easier. In 1882 the United States Congress passed the CHINESE EXCLUSION ACT, which prohibited laborers from China and countries across Asia from immigrating into the country. This was the first law that stopped people with a specific ETHNICITY from coming into the country. The Chinese Exclusion Act made it impossible for many people from Asia to move to the United States. Immigrants from Asian countries and their families were not able to become United States citizens until 1943. The Chinese Exclusion Act was unfair and unjust. The government misused and abused its power to exclude a lot of people because of their ethnicities and nationalities.

DID YOU KNOW?

1865

After SLAVERY became outlawed in the United States in 1865, a lot of cities and states created rules and laws that made it really hard for Black and Brown people to be able to do a lot of things. They were not able to vote. Black people were not able to own homes and property. In some places Black people were not able to go wherever they wanted to or whenever they wanted to. There were rules that said Black people had to be home at a certain time, and they were not allowed to be outside at night. It was not safe for Black people to be out at night. Many of the rules and laws that were put in place made it so that there were a lot of places that were unsafe for Black people to go. Those rules were called the JIM CROW LAWS. The Jim Crow Laws became a part of our society.

1920s + 1930s

In the 1920s and 1930s, the United States removed up to two million people of Mexican DESCENT (many of them were American citizens) from the country. (Descent means being related to your ancestors. If you are of Mexican descent, your ancestors are from México.) The United States was going through a time when business and trade were not good and many people did not have jobs. In some parts of the country, white Americans were prejudiced and discriminated against Mexican Americans, blaming them for taking their jobs. (They did not.) Some state, city, and town governments forced their Mexican and Mexican American citizens to leave and blocked them from returning. The forced deportations (removal) of people of Mexican descent were unfair and unjust. The governments misused and abused their power by making it so people were not able to return to their homes or jobs, and families were kept apart.

1942

On February 19, 1942, soon after the bombing of Pearl Harbor during World War II, the United States president Franklin D. Roosevelt signed an executive order that forced many Japanese American citizens, people of Japanese descent, and Japanese immigrants living on the west coast of the country to be put into INTERNMENT CAMPS. An internment camp is a prison. The government demanded that they leave their homes, places of work, schools, neighborhoods, and everything they knew to go to one of ten prison camps. About 120,000 people were held against their will because the government saw them as a threat to the country. (They were not!) These prison camps were unfair and unjust. The government misused and abused their power and made it so thousands of Japanese Americans and Japanese people living in the United States were discriminated against, their homes and businesses were taken from them, and they were treated as prisoners because of where they and their ancestors were from.

WHAT ARE SOME MORE WAYS INSTITUTIONS USE THEIR POWER TO HELP RACISM GROW?

When institutions misuse and abuse their power to oppress People of the Global Majority, it is racism. This is how institutions help keep racism going and help racism to grow.

Some schools and places where people work will not allow people to wear some hairstyles that are worn by Black people (like locs, natural hair, and braids). These hairstyles do not fit into the dominant culture. The workplaces and schools that do not allow these hairstyles want people to look more like the members of the dominant culture. This is an abuse of power toward Black people. This is not okay. It is unfair and unjust to have a rule that asks some people to change their hair to look more like the people who are in the dominant culture.

Do you remember how some people from Europe made up reasons why it was okay to enslave, hurt, and oppress People of the Global Majority? Some of the reasons they came up with turned into stereotypes that are still believed today! Some people who were members of the dominant culture wanted to believe that Black people were better able to do long, hard, tiring work outside and that white people did not need to do these things. Another thing they believed was that Black people do not feel pain as much as white people. This is not true. Pain is something that is felt by almost everyone. Some doctors and nurses still believe that Black people do not feel pain. This is a hurtful stereotype to believe because some doctors and nurses still treat Black patients differently. They do not believe that they are really hurt and in pain. This is not okay. This is an abuse of power.

The planned misuse and abuse of power by institutions that happens over and over again has really helped to keep racism growing. Racism has stayed a part of our lives every day for so long. The planned misuse and abuse of power by institutions has also kept the people who are members of the dominant culture in power for a very long time.

THINK ABOUT IT!

Can you think of other ways institutions misuse and abuse their power?

WHAT iS ANTiRACISM?

Antiracism is making a choice to be active and resist racism.

For as long as there has been racism, there has been antiracism. There have always been people working for justice and fighting against racism.

To RESIST means to not give in and to stand up and sit tall against someone or something. Resisting racism means you are against racism. You will challenge racism, stand up, sit tall, speak out, and use your power against it.

An antiracist person believes that Indigenous, Black, Latine, and Asian People of the Global Majority are human and their lives matter.

An antiracist person wants to dismantle racism so it no longer exists. An antiracist person will work with others to end racism.

Racism will not go away on its own.

We have to work together for more just and fair communities where the color of our skin does not decide who we will become.

HOW DOES RACISM AFFECT OUR LiVES?

Racism is everywhere.

Racism is in every town, city, state, and country.

Racism is in hospitals and schools, museums and libraries.

Racism is at the parks and aquariums.

Racism has caused a lot of stress and hurt for everyone, especially Indigenous and Black People of the Global Majority.

Racism is in the rules and laws of our society.

Racism has become a part of every institution in the United States.

Racism has made life much harder than it needs to be for Black, Indigenous, Latine, and Asian People of the Global Majority.

Racism is a negative thing in our lives. It is not okay.

Racism hurts everyone!

WHAT DOES IT MEAN WHEN SOMEONE IS PREJUDiCED?

PREJUDICE is a belief, attitude, or feeling about a person or group of people. Prejudice comes from not having all of the right information. Prejudices come from no real reasons or thoughts or experiences.

Everyone has prejudices.

Sometimes prejudice can be good.

Most of the time prejudice can be bad.

People can have prejudice against people who have a different skin color from their own. They can have a negative belief, attitude, or feeling about people who are a different race than they are.

Sometimes it can be really clear when someone is acting prejudiced against another person or a group of people. Prejudice shows up in the words people use, how they act, and what they do. They may act unkind and say and do things that make other people hurt and upset.

Someone who has prejudice might say something mean to you about the color of your skin or about the way your hair looks and feels.

A person who has prejudice against people with darker skin might move their body away from yours. They might tease or bully you.

This is not okay.

But sometimes it is not very clear or easy to know when someone is acting prejudiced and racist.

A person who is prejudiced might say or do something that makes you feel uncomfortable, but other people might think it is okay and normal.

Someone who has prejudice against people with darker skin might always say nicer things about white people or people with lighter skin. They might say something to you that makes you feel upset and like you are not important.

This is not okay.

HOW DO i KNOW WHEN SOMEONE IS ACTiNG PREJUDICED?

You will not always know when someone is acting prejudiced toward you.

Sometimes it is really clear when someone has prejudice. Sometimes it is not very clear when someone has prejdudice.

Trust yourself! You can also always ask people you trust to help you out!

> TRUST is believing in yourself and others. Trust is when you know people will do what they tell you they will do, and you believe they are telling you the truth.
>
> Why is trust important? Trust can help us to feel safe and able to be our whole selves. It helps us to feel connected to other people so we can live and work in communities together. When there is trust, people feel ready to help one another.

WHAT ARE MICROAGGRESSiONS?

Microaggressions are a kind of discrimination. They seem small, but they are not! Microaggressions are negative words and actions from people who are members of the dominant culture toward people who are not part of the dominant culture.

Microaggressions happen a lot.

They come from lots of different people who are members of the dominant culture.

Every negative word and action hurts.

Each time a microaggression happens, it feels like a paper cut. (Paper cuts are small but, wow, do they hurt!)

Every negative word and action feels like a new paper cut in the same spot. It really hurts, and the pain feels worse and worse.

Microaggressions can make you feel small. They can make you not believe in yourself. Microaggressions will leave you feeling sad, uncomfortable, and hurt. Microaggressions are not okay.

Here are some examples of microaggressions:

I get asked "What are you?" all the time. The people who ask me are trying to learn more about my race and ethnicity. They want to see if I am like them or not. That question, "What are you?" is rude. I don't like it. It makes me feel like I don't belong. My race and ethnicity are none of their business!

At school, anytime we read books that have Black characters in them, my teacher asks me to talk about them. My teacher does this with the other Black kids too, but they don't ask kids who are not Black to talk about the Black characters in the books. I think my teachers think I am only important when we are reading about Black people. I am important all the time!

A lot of people use the wrong PRONOUN when talking to me and about me. It is not okay. It makes me feel sad and like I don't matter. When my friends and I correct them, they will still misgender me. That makes me feel even worse. It is not okay for people to use the wrong pronouns!

WHaT You CaN Do!

WHAT DO I DO WHEN SOMEONE IS ACTiNg PREJUDICED TOWARD ME?

When someone is acting prejudiced toward you, you can go to a person you trust and tell them.

The person you trust might be a parent or caregiver, a friend, your librarian, your grandparent or cousin—it could be anyone. It could also be a group of people who share some identities or experiences with you and understand what it is like to have those identities and experiences.

You know who you trust.

Telling someone else will help you to not hold in all of the hurt, and they can help you.

When someone is acting prejudiced toward you, you can speak out and stand up and tell them that what they are doing is not okay. (To learn more about how to **advocate** for yourself, see the next page!) You can ask other people (like your friends and family) to support you and help you advocate for yourself too.

> To ADVOCATE means to support or help yourself and others. An advocate is someone who supports others by sharing their power, speaking up, writing letters of support, arguing on behalf of others, and promoting a cause.

It is never okay for someone to act prejudiced toward you.

It is never okay for someone to discriminate against you.

No one is more important than anyone else.

It is not okay for some people to make others feel like they are not important.

It is never okay for anyone (whether it be one person or a whole institution) to get away with hurting you.

If someone is acting prejudiced toward you, if they are discriminating against you, if they are hurting you, **_please tell an adult you trust as soon as you can!_**

HOW DO I ADVOCATE FOR MYSELF?

Advocating for yourself is not an easy thing to do.

Letting other people know what you are thinking and feeling is not an easy thing to do.

First, believe in yourself.

It is never okay for anyone to make you feel small.

It is never okay for anyone to make you feel like you are not important.

It is never okay for anyone to tell you to be silent and ignore you.

Know why you are standing up. Know what you are advocating for.

Take a deep breath before you say something. Take the time you need to figure out what it is you want to say.

Sometimes you will know what you want to say. Sometimes you will not.

You can start by saying something like  *and*  *It is okay to say*

Trust yourself.

Do not give up.

Remember that you can ask for help too!

You are not alone.

You never have to do this by yourself.

You can call on a friend, a caregiver, or anyone you trust when you need it.

There are people in your life who want to help you!

Have you ever heard of an "I" statement?

An "I" statement is when you talk about yourself. You describe yourself and your experience and not anyone else.

You can say something like "I feel _____" and "I noticed that _____" and "I am not okay because _____." Using an "I" statement is important when you are standing up and advocating for yourself. It makes the person you are talking to listen to you because you are sharing how you feel and what you noticed. Using a statement like "You did _____" or "You made me feel _____" can put the person you are talking to on the defense, and they will be less likely to really hear what you are saying.

You can practice using an "I" statement anytime!

I FEEL _confused_.

I NOTICED THAT _my friends move away from me when I shout_

I AM NOT OKAY BECAUSE _I am not getting the help I need in class_.

Everyone has prejudices.

If you are acting prejudiced toward someone, you will need to stop being prejudiced.

If you made someone else feel bad and hurt, you will need to **repair** with them.

> To REPAIR with someone means that you will work to make things better. You take responsibility for how you hurt the other person. You admit you did something wrong, listen to the person who is hurt, and work to make sure you don't hurt them again.

How do you know you have prejudice against someone? Here are some things you might do:

You might share a stereotype that is not true or laugh at a racist joke.

You might say something that is biased and negative.

You might do something that hurts someone else's body or feelings.

None of these are okay.

If you are acting prejudiced toward someone and you made another person feel bad and hurt, you will need to admit what you did and that it was not okay.

You have to say something to begin the repair. Do not be quiet and do nothing.

It is important to admit what you did, that it was not okay, and to apologize to the person you hurt.

You can admit that you were in the wrong and tell them that you will not do it again. (You can really work on making sure you will not make them feel bad and hurt them again!)

The person you were acting prejudiced toward and unkind to will need some time. They may need some time and space away from you. Please give them that time and space.

Repair takes time.

When you work on repairing with someone, you will need to admit you were in the wrong.

Listen to the person who was hurt. Make sure that what happened does not happen again.

You can change.

Do not act prejudiced toward people.

CAN I REPAIR WITH MYSELF TOO?

You can repair too.

It does not feel good to have prejudice against other people.

It does not feel good to make other people feel sad and hurt.

It is important that you repair with yourself too.

You can check in with yourself!

When you are the person who made someone else feel bad and hurt, you need to think about what happened and what you did.

You can think about why you did what you did.

You can notice what effect stereotypes and biases had on you.

Did you believe in things that are not true?

Understand your own feelings and know that you may have been acting out of fear and not knowing the truth about people who are different from you.

You can spend some time making a plan to not have prejudice against people. Ask your friends and people you trust to help you out.

When you work on repairing with others and yourself, you can get information and learn the truth.

You can also learn more about how prejudice and racism have been around for a long time.

You can learn about the history of our country, so you do not do the same things again.

When you spend time repairing with yourself, you can get a better understanding of what happened and really work to make sure it does not happen again.

IS RACISM MORE THAN PERSONAL PREJUDICE AND BIAS?

A lot of times when people think about racism, they think only about the personal prejudice part. It is the one part that affects everyone right away.

You can see it and hear it.

You know what personal prejudice feels like and looks like.

People can do something about it right away. You can change your biases and prejudices.

There is more to racism than just the personal prejudice part. Racism is *both* personal prejudice and bias *and* the planned misuse and abuse of power by institutions.

Both parts of racism affect all of our lives in a very real and hurtful way every day.

REMEMBER:

An institution is an organized group of people working together. Institutions have existed for a long time. The people in an institution change, but the institution does not change much. Institutions help to make rules, laws, and traditions for people in society.

Institutions are a part of everyone's lives.

You go to schools. You shop at stores and businesses. You go see doctors and dentists. You watch television and movies, read books, and live in homes.

People are a part of institutions, and institutions are a part of everyone's lives.

Institutions have a lot of power.

When institutions misuse and abuse their power, it is oppression.

When they use their power to oppress Black, Indigenous, and all People of the Global Majority, it is not okay—it is racism.

HOW CAN I SPOT INJUSTICE?

You can spot injustice.

Use all of your senses to notice the world around you!

Spend time paying attention to what is around you.

Spend time paying attention to yourself.

Be curious and ask questions about what you see and hear.

You will be able to spot injustice.

How do you feel inside?

Does your stomach hurt?

Is your heart beating really fast?

Do you feel hot and sweaty?

Do you want to run far away?

Do your feet feel like they are trapped in quicksand?

Sometimes you can feel injustice before you see it.

It will make you want to run. Or, it might make you freeze in place.

Injustice does not feel good.

You might notice injustice right away. You also might need some time to think about what it is you just saw or heard and what just happened. It is okay to take a little time to figure out what you noticed.

You can also talk to your friends, family, and people in your community about what you notice. They probably are noticing the same things as you!

THINK ABOUT IT!

You can ask yourself some questions to help you figure out what you noticed. Here are some questions you might want to ask:

What is happening?

Who is it happening to?

Who is doing the hurting?

Is someone being biased or prejudiced?

Is someone sharing a stereotype and the wrong information?

Is someone being prejudiced toward another person or a group of people?

Is an institution discriminating against people?

Is there a rule or law that makes unfair and unjust treatment okay?

Is this something that keeps happening?

Is something being done to stop this injustice?

HOW DO i TALK ABOUT RACISM AND INJUSTiCE WITH PEOPLE?

Talking about racism and injustice is not an easy thing to do.

Sometimes you will not have the words you want to talk about racism.

Sometimes you might worry that the people you are talking to will not always believe you.

When you talk about racism and injustice, tell the truth.

Share what you noticed and ask questions.

Talk about why you believe what happened was an act of racism and injustice.

You can even use the definitions of racism and oppression to help you. You can share them with others. (Remember, racism is personal prejudice and bias and the planned misuse and abuse of power by institutions.)

Practice talking about injustice. Always share the truth and what you noticed. Tell the facts. Be clear with what you are sharing.

It is okay to fidget and cry, and move around.

It is okay to take a break if you need to.

It may also help to practice talking with people you know and trust (like your friends, a parent or caregiver, a family member, teacher, coach, etc.) before you share your truth and open up. You can even practice sharing with your stuffed animals!

To help you to start talking about racism and injustice, you can say something like, "I just noticed something that was not okay." Then share what you noticed.

You might also want to write things down before you feel you are ready to talk about them.

Your friends can help you out too! Talking with them about what you noticed can help. They might share what they noticed too.

The more you practice talking about racism and injustice, the easier talking about racism, oppression, and injustice with others will become!

Racism and injustice are everywhere and affect us all.

Be ready to notice and talk about racism and injustice. The more you notice racism and injustice, and the more you talk about it, the better we become at dismantling racism!

PuTTiNG IT ALL ToGeTHeR

✳ Fair means everyone gets what they need. Your identities and your experiences help you to understand what is fair and what is not.

✳ Justice means being fair. Justice is something that happens when people are treated fairly. It is when every person gets what they need to be healthy, cared for, and safe.

✳ Equal means having the same amount of something. What is equal is not always what is fair.

✳ A bias is a belief about a person, a group of people, a place, or a thing. Everyone has biases. Usually, your biases are hidden. You are not always aware of what biases you have. Bias can change.

✳ Prejudice is a belief, attitude, or feeling about a person or group of people. Everyone has prejudices. Prejudices come from the stereotypes and biases you have. Unlike your biases, usually you and other people are aware of your prejudices. Prejudices can change.

✳ Discrimination is the unfair and unequal treatment of people. It is hurtful. Discrimination is not okay.

✳ Unjust means something is not fair. Injustice is when something is unfair and unjust.

✳ Power is having control over yourself and the freedom to make choices and change. People and institutions have power.

✳ An institution is an organized group of people working together.

✳ Schools, hospitals, banks, prisons, businesses and stores, government, media and entertainment, and places of worship are all institutions.

✳ Institutions help to make traditions, rules, and laws that affect people, communities, and society.

✳ Everyone has power! Not everyone is welcomed, encouraged, or asked to use their power.

＊ Some people have more power than others in this country. People who are members of the dominant culture of our country have A LOT of power.

＊ Oppression is a word used to describe when power is misused and abused and it happens on purpose. Oppression is unfair and unjust. It has a negative effect on people and society.

＊ There are many different kinds of oppression. They are usually directed toward people with social identities that are not the same as the ones people in the dominant culture have.

＊ Ableism is when people with disabilities are oppressed.

＊ Ageism is when children, teenagers, and elderly people are oppressed.

＊ Cissexism is when transgender people, nonbinary people, and everyone who does not identify as female or male are oppressed.

＊ Classism is when people who are living in poverty, people who are experiencing homelessness, and people who do not have a lot of resources and money are oppressed.

＊ Heterosexism is when people who are in the LGBTQQIP2AA+ community are oppressed.

＊ Racism is when Black, Indigenous, Asian, and Latine People of the Global Majority are oppressed.

＊ Sexism is when women and people who do not identify as male are oppressed.

＊ Intersectionality is a word used to help people understand that anyone can have more than just one identity at any one time. It also helps us to understand that some parts of a person's identity may give them power.

＊ Racism is personal prejudice and bias *and* the planned misuse and abuse of power by institutions. It is the unfair and unjust treatment of People of the Global Majority based on the idea that white people are better.

* No one person invented racism. It has been around for hundreds and hundreds of years.

* In the 1700s, a social ranking was created that put people in society into different groups. These groups were based on the color of people's skin, their facial features, and where they and their ancestors were from.

* Racism was created by white people from Europe, and it was used to make Black, Indigenous, and all People of the Global Majority seem like they were less human.

* Institutions help racism grow. They help to make sure that the dominant culture is everywhere in the United States.

* When institutions misuse and abuse their power to oppress People of the Global Majority, it is racism. This is how institutions help keep racism going and help racism to grow.

* Antiracism is making a choice to be active and resist racism.

* An antiracist person believes that Indigenous, Black, Latine, and Asian People of the Global Majority are human and their lives matter. They work together with other antiracist people to dismantle racism.

* Racism hurts everyone!

* You will not always know when someone is acting prejudiced against you.

* Microaggressions are a kind of discrimination. They seem small, but they are not. Microaggressions are negative words and actions from people who are members of the dominant culture. Microaggressions happen a lot, and they hurt.

* If someone is acting prejudiced against you, if they are discriminating against you, if they are hurting you, please tell an adult you trust as soon as you can!

* Advocating for yourself is not an easy thing to do. Believe in yourself.

✳ If someone says you are acting prejudiced, you probably are. You can work on repairing with them and work to make sure you are not acting prejudiced again.

✳ You can repair with yourself too.

✳ There is more to racism than just the personal prejudice part. Racism is both personal prejudice and bias *and* the planned misuse and abuse of power by institutions.

✳ You can spot injustice! Use all of your senses to notice the world around you.

✳ When you talk about racism and injustice, tell the truth.

✳ Racism and injustice are everywhere and affect us all! Be ready to notice and talk about racism and injustice. The more you notice racism and injustice, and the more you talk about it, the better we become at dismantling racism!

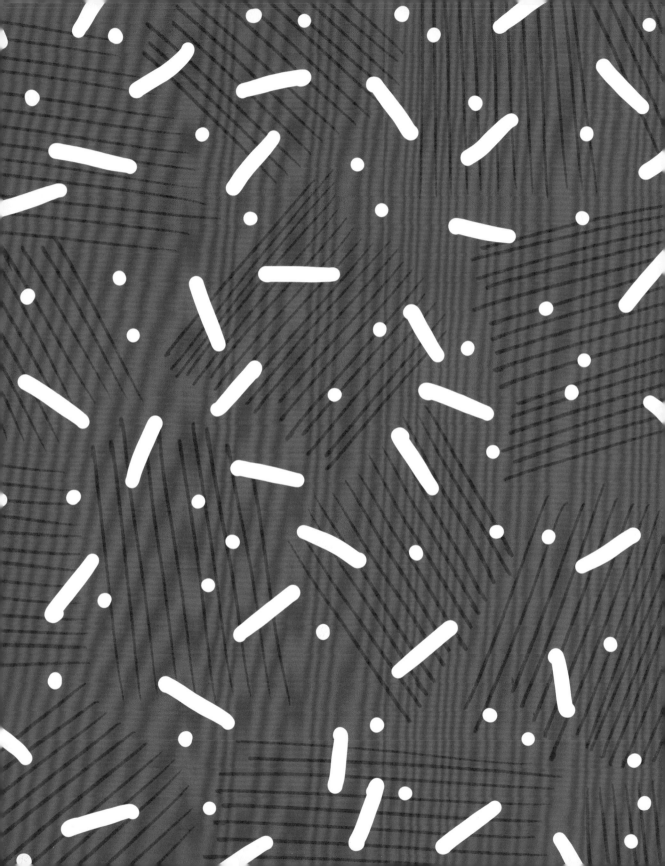

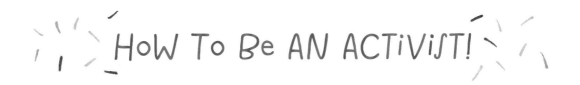

HoW To Be AN ACTiViST!

WHAT IS ACTIVISM?

Activism is taking action against injustice.

Activism is working to make positive change in your community and society.

You are working to change society so it is more fair and just for everyone.

Here are some of the things you might be questioning and want to change:

Why do some people have a lot more money than other people?

Why is it okay for some teachers and schools to treat Black and Brown students differently from white students?

Why are white families more likely to own their own homes than Black and Brown families?

Why is it okay for lawmakers to decide who gets to use which bathrooms in schools? (Why can't students choose for themselves?)

How can we work together to end climate change?

Why do some communities have dirty and unsafe drinking water and others have clean and safe drinking water?

What are some things you want to work for and change?

IS COMMUNITY SERVICE THE SAME AS ACTIVISM?

You might have done some community service before. Community service is when you work to help people in your community with things they need right away.

Community service can be great!

Some of the things people do for their community are collecting food, raising money to help people pay for the things they need, and collecting outdoor clothing for kids who do not have boots and jackets.

Community service can be really helpful to people in the community and society.

Activism and community service are different.

Community service helps people right away, which is great! You and your friends might bake cookies and sell them to raise some money for your local animal shelter.

Activism is working to change the big problems in society like racism, classism, and other oppression. You might work with people in your neighborhood to try to change some of the rules and laws in your community that are unfair and unjust.

Community service and activism are not the same thing. They both help your community. Community service is something you can do to help people in your community right away with some of the things they need. Activism is something you can do to help the people in your community to end racism and oppression.

CAN I BE AN ACTIVIST?

Yes! You can be an activist!

An activist is someone who takes action against injustice.

You can take action on your own or with people in your community.

There is no one right way to be active. There are many different ways you can be an activist.

You will find ways to be active that work for you and your community that have positive lasting change!

HOW CAN I BE AN ACTIVIST?

There are many different ways you can be an activist.

You will find ways to be active that work best for you and your community.

Here are some of the things you can do!

You can WRITE POSTCARDS AND LETTERS to some of the people who make rules and laws in your community and in the United States. You can help change the rules and laws so they are more fair and just. Tell them what you would like to change and why it is important to you. (You can call their offices too!)

You can BOYCOTT STORES AND BUSINESSES that discriminate against People of the Global Majority. Boycott means you will no longer go to the stores or buy things from them because it is not okay that they discriminate against people.

You can get together with some of your friends, other kids at school, and kids in your neighborhood. Together, you can START A GROUP OR CLUB around social justice.

You can **GO TO PROTESTS** and marches with your family and friends. You will be with other people in your community who care about ending racism and injustice.

You can **MAKE SIGNS** with your family and friends that share what you believe in. Your signs could say things like "Black Lives Matter," "Protect Our Earth!" and "¡Nadie Es Ilegal!" You can let people in your community know what you believe. You can put the signs up in your windows, in your yard, on the door, and other places where people can see them every day.

You can open up, **SHARE YOUR VOICE**, your words, your thoughts, and ideas because they need to be known! You can talk with your friends, other kids in your school, and people in your neighborhood! You can talk about the things that are unfair and unjust. Make sure you listen to what People of the Global Majority have to say too.

Can you think of other ways to take action and be an activist?

Even something that may feel small can have a big positive change!

Activism is for everyone.

HOW DO i ADVOCATE FOR OTHER PEOPLE?

You can **advocate** for yourself and for other people too!

When you notice injustice, you will want to do something about it!

It is important not to jump right into what you think needs to be done.

You will need to take a little time to notice what is happening and to listen to the people around you. The people you want to advocate and stand up for will already have an idea of what needs to be done. They are the people you need to listen to.

REMEMBER:

To ADVOCATE means to support or help yourself and others. An advocate is someone who supports others by sharing their power, speaking up, writing letters of support, arguing on behalf of others, and promoting a cause.

Do you remember some of the different ways you can be an activist? You can write letters and postcards to the people who make rules and laws in your community. You can go to protests with other people. You can boycott stores and businesses that discriminate against People of the Global Majority. There are so many ways you can take action to make change. These are also ways you can advocate for yourself and the people in your community and in society!

Advocating for yourself and others usually means you will need to use your **power**, share your words, and use your voice however you can. Be a champion for change!

Be loud!

When you advocate for other people, make sure you do not use your voice to speak for someone unless they want you to. You can ask them, "Do you want me to say something?"

You will also want to make sure you are not using your words to talk over the people you are standing up and advocating for. Use whatever you can to help **amplify** others!

When you help to AMPLIFY someone's words, thoughts, ideas, and actions, you are helping them to be louder, to be heard, to be seen, to take up space!

It is important to advocate for other people, because you care about the people you are in community with and because you want to make positive change together!

ACCOUNTABILITY is a word you will hear a lot in activism. Accountability means to take responsibility for yourself. You are in charge of what you say and what you do.

Accountability means you understand that what you say and do has an effect on others.

You are in charge of you, the things you say, and the things you do.

Accountability is important because it helps to build TRUST with the people in your community.

The people you are standing up and advocating with will need to be able to trust you, and you will need to trust them. You will work together and do what is best for your community and society!

When you and the people you are taking action with trust one another, you will be able to make positive change!

You will want to make sure that you are listening and learning about what is best for the people who are most affected by racism and oppression. You are working to do what is best for your community, not just for yourself.

HOW CAN I TALK TO OTHER PEOPLE ABOUT RACISM?

It's great that you want to talk to other people about racism and oppression!

There are many different ways you can advocate for justice and against racism.

Talking to your family and friends, the people in your school and neighborhood, and people in your community is important.

Tell the truth and share what you know about racism. Share the facts with anyone and everyone who will listen!

You can ask questions too. This is how we learn!

When talking about injustice, talk about what is fair and just.

Remember—racism is personal **prejudice** and **bias** and the planned misuse and abuse of power by **institutions**.

You can get good information to share from activists in your community. They are working to **dismantle** racism and oppression every day.

Books and some news sources are good places to get information too.

You can learn more about racism and its history in our country and share what you are learning with other people. You can talk about how racism affects People of the Global Majority. You can talk about how racism hurts everyone.

The more you know and share with others, the better you can work for a more fair and just community.

HOW CAN I WORK ON ANTIRACISM WITH OTHER PEOPLE MY AGE?

You can start an **antiracist** group!

You can do this at your school, your local library, your community center, where you worship, or with other people in your neighborhood.

An antiracist group can be a good way for you to get to know other antiracist kids (and adults). You can use the time together to learn from each other and plan how to take action for positive antiracist change in your community.

You will need the help of an adult, like a caregiver, teacher, counselor, or librarian. They will be able to help the antiracist group find a space where you can meet. The adult will also be able to help you find materials and resources that you may need. You and the adult you are working with will find a time that is best for the antiracist group to meet. If the antiracist group is at school, you might be able to meet at lunchtime. After school can be a time that works well for a lot of people too.

The first time the antiracist group meets, you will want to spend some time getting to know everyone. When everyone gets to know each other, you will start to trust in your antiracist group. You will also want to make some boundaries about how you will all be when you are together.

Your antiracist group will be able to plan how you will take action to dismantle racism. You will be working together to build a more fair and just antiracist community!

A BOUNDARY is a rule or a limit that you set for yourself. You can have one boundary or many boundaries.

Boundaries help you to know when to take a break.

You can make boundaries for yourself. You can make some boundaries about when and how you will advocate for yourself. Your boundaries can also be about when you will ask others for help. You get to decide what your boundaries are.

If someone does not respect your boundaries, they are not ready to work with you. You do not have to work with someone who will not respect you. It is okay for you to walk away.

Here is an example of a boundary:

You can have a boundary about not letting anyone touch you. Other people need to ask you if it is okay to give you a hug, touch your arm, or hold your hand.

You can share this boundary with others by saying something like "I do not like being hugged without being asked first. Please ask me before you hug me."

USING YOUR "VOICE"

WHAT DO I DO IF NO ONE WILL LISTEN TO ME?

There will be times when no one will listen to you.

They may not want to hear what you have to say about racism and injustice.

Both kids and adults may not want to hear what you have to say.

Just because they will not listen to you does not mean you should be quiet. What you have to say is important!

Not everyone believes that racism is a problem. They may not be ready to hear what you have to say. They may not want to learn about racism. Some people will choose to not know that racism is real. They will choose to be quiet.

Talking about racism and injustice is hard!

It is something that makes people really uncomfortable. This is mostly because they do not have the facts and understand what racism is. They may not know how racism has been a part of our country for a really, really long time.

Even when no one will pay attention or listen—keep using your voice, sharing your words, and making your beliefs known.

KEEP SPEAKING UP
AND ADVOCATING EVEN WHEN
NO ONE IS LISTENING
OR PAYING ATTENTION.

You and the adults in your life will not always agree on all the same things. Sometimes it will be small things, like what time you go to bed. Other times it will be something big, like how you understand the world and care for your community.

This is hard because you may want your caregivers to care about the same things you do. The people in your life will not always believe in the same things as you. You cannot change what other people think, but you can always share with them.

Share who you are with the people in your life!

Are you able to find people you know and can trust who will listen to you and support you?

Who are the people you are thinking of? Maybe one of your teachers or a librarian is some-one you can trust.

Do you have some family members who you can talk to about the things you believe in? Maybe your neighbors or one of your sports coaches is someone you trust. You may be able to talk to one of your friends' parents or a neighbor too!

Any time you start to feel unsafe (like if someone tries to hurt you, makes you watch or listen to things that go against what you believe in, or if they keep you away from your friends and other people who think like you), tell someone you trust right away!

WHAT DO I DO iF I AM NOT MAKiNG A DIFFERENCE?

THERE WILL BE TIMES WHEN YOU FEEL LIKE YOU ARE NOT MAKING A DIFFERENCE.

Take a moment and notice yourself and the community around you.

How has your community changed?

How have you changed?

KNOW THAT YOU ARE!

YOU ARE HELPING TO DISMANTLE RACISM.

YOU ARE HELPING TO MAKE POSITIVE CHANGE IN SOCIETY!

EVEN THE SMALLEST ACTION CAN HAVE A BIG EFFECT FOR POSITIVE CHANGE!

WHO ELSE IS RESISTING RACISM?

There are many people in your community and in our country who also advocate against racism and injustice just like you! The more you learn about becoming antiracist, the closer you will become with the people in your community.

There are people in your own community, in your schools, hospitals, places of worship, and in your cities and towns who are working to dismantle racism. There are people everywhere who are doing this work! There are young people just like you who are **resisting** and advocating against racism, and it is amazing!

Here are some antiracist people we are learning about:

Thandiwe Abdullah is an activist from California and uses any PRONOUNS. They started attending protests when they were two. When she was a young teen, Thandiwe started the Black Lives Matter Youth Vanguard with other activists. This was a few years after Patrisse Cullors, Alicia Garza, and Opal Tometi started the Black Lives Matter Movement. Thandiwe also worked to make Black Lives Matter in Schools, which is being used in schools across the country. Thandiwe is working for a more just society without racism and oppression!

They said, "I think we should be leading the work of dreaming of something better for ourselves."

Thandiwe Abdullah inspires me to get together and work with people who care about and believe that Black lives matter!

Charitie Ropati is an activist from the Native Village of Kongiganak, in Alaska, and uses she/her pronouns. She is an advocate for INDIGENOUS students and their right to wear traditional and sacred clothing (also called cultural regalia) at school graduation ceremonies. Charitie is working to change the way schools teach only the DOMINANT CULTURE of the United States. It is not okay that Native American people and their history are left out of the country's history.

Charitie Ropati inspires me to learn more about myself and my ANCESTORS and to question what we don't learn about at school.

Juwaria Jama is an activist from Minnesota who is standing up for the environment. They are fighting for environmental justice. The work they are doing shows us that People of the Global Majority and people who are not members of the dominant culture are most affected by climate change. Juwaria Jama asks lawmakers in their state, the country, and the world to put their money and resources toward protecting people and the environment.

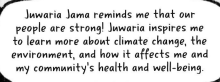

Juwaria Jama reminds me that our people are strong! Juwaria inspires me to learn more about climate change, the environment, and how it affects me and my community's health and well-being.

Some of the other young people who inspire us every day are:

FeeLiNG GRaTeFuL!

We are always grateful for the many ancestors who have been doing the work of **antiracism** and fighting for justice for decades and centuries! We are here because of them and we will keep working for an antiracist society together because of them.

PuTTiNG IT ALL ToGeTHeR

✳ You are becoming an antiracist kid!

✳ Activism is taking action against injustice. It is working to make positive change in your community and society.

✳ Community service and activism are not the same thing. They both help your community. Community service is something you can do to help people in your community right away with some of the things they need. Activism is something you can do to help the people in your community to end racism and oppression.

✳ You can be an activist!

✳ There is no one right way to be active. There are many different ways you can be an activist.

✳ Some of the ways you can be an activist:

  ✳ You can write letters and postcards to the people who make rules and laws in your community.

  ✳ You can go to protests with other people.

  ✳ You can boycott stores and businesses that discriminate against People of the Global Majority.

  ✳ There are so many ways you can take action to make change.

✳ You can advocate for yourself and you can advocate for other people too!

✳ Be loud! Take up space!

✳ Help amplify someone's words, thoughts, ideas, and actions.

* Accountability is important because it helps to build trust with the people in your community. The people you are advocating with will need to be able to trust you and you will need to trust them. You will work together and do what is best for your community and society!

* Tell the truth and share what you know about racism. Share the facts with anyone and everyone who will listen!

* You can start an antiracist group for people your age and people in your community!

* Even when no one will listen or pay attention—keep using your voice, sharing your words, and making your beliefs known! Keep advocating even when no one is listening or paying attention!

* The people in your life will not always believe in the same things as you. You cannot change what other people think, but you can always share with them.

* There are people in your own community, in your schools, hospitals, places of worship, and in your cities and towns who are working to dismantle racism. There are people everywhere who are doing this work! There are young people just like you who are resisting and advocating against racism, and it is amazing!

You ARe BeCoMiNG aN ANTiRaCiJT KiD!

You picked up this book.

You know **racism** exists and that it is **unfair** and **unjust**.

You believe the lives of **Black, Indigenous, Asian**, and **Latine People of the Global Majority** matter and are important.

You are starting to notice **prejudice, stereotypes**, and racism.

You are starting to be a champion for change.

You know how to take action.

You are learning and growing every day.

You are a part of a big **community** of people working together to dismantle racism and **oppression**.

You are making your **ancestors** proud!

ACKNoWLeDGMeNTS

This is always one of my favorite parts of books! This acknowledgments section is where I get to thank all of the people who helped me make this book possible!

There are so many people I have to thank!

Thank you for believing in me.

Thank you for seeing me.

Thank you for showing me that my voice matters.

Thank you for answering emails, random DMs, and late-night texts.

Thank you for passing your excitement on to me.

Thank you for listening to me.

Thank you for dreaming with me.

Thank you—Kwame Alexander, Ayesha Pande (and the whole crew), Christine Platt, Amelia Allen Sherwood, Britt Hawthorne, Trisha Moquino, Antonia Adams, Keiran Slattery, Liz Kleinrock, Katie Kitchens, Lorena Germán, and to everyone who has reminded me I am a whole person.

Weslie Turner, my editor, and the Versify crew—thank you!

Thank you to the authenticity readers for your care and guidance.

Of course, I am grateful to my mom and my twin—for their constant and unwavering support always. TJ and Mom, I love you. To my nephew, KJ, who thinks I'm a superhero and to his mama, AV, for not correcting him—I love you. To JS, SS, MC, and MC, thank you for helping to entertain the kiddos so I could make some deadlines.

And, to my husband: thank you for all the things, from the weekends, to endless cups of afternoon tea, to cookies with pink frosting—I love you. To my most favorite kiddos in the world, J and S. Thank you for always asking big questions, being patient with me, sharing hugs, and being my biggest fans! (I'm yours!) I love you!

Thank you to all the students and educators at JSS school! I loved spending the pandemic school year with you and am grateful for your trust, enthusiasm, and honesty.

Thank you to all of my former students. This book grew out of all the work we did together over the past two decades. You helped me to truly see that antiracism is not just something for the adults. Thank you for trusting me and for trusting yourselves.

And lastly, I thank and honor the ancestors who came before me and paved the way to where I am today. I am because of you.

ABouT the AuTHoR aND ILLuJTRaToR

Photo © James Azar Salem

Tiffany Jewell is a Black biracial writer, twin sister, first-generation American, cisgender mama, anti-bias antiracist (ABAR) educator, and consultant. She is the author of the #1 *New York Times* and #1 Indie bestseller *This Book Is Anti-Racist*. Tiffany lives on the homeland of the Pocumtuc and the Nipmuck with her two young storytellers, husband, a turtle she's had since she was nine years old, and a small dog with a big personality. Find her online at anti-biasmontessori.com and on Twitter and Instagram at @tiffanymjewell.

Nicole Miles is an American illustrator from the Bahamas currently living in West Yorkshire, United Kingdom, with her pet snake and human boyfriend. Her favorite forms of procrastiworking are bettering her hand-lettering, making animated GIFs, chronicling silly life moments or informative sustainability tips in comic form, experimenting with film photography, or sewing new garments for herself. But she also dedicates a lot of time to improving her second language (French), reading, and, recently, going on forest walks. Find her online at nicolemillo.com and on Instagram at @nicolemillo.

Photo © Daniel Hamilton

GLOSSARY

ableism: Discrimination and oppression against people who have visible or not visible physical, emotional, or neurological and mental disabilities

accountability: Taking responsibility for yourself

activism: Taking action against injustice

activist: Someone who takes action against injustice

advocate: To support or help yourself and others

affirmation: A positive sentence, word, or phrase that can help you remember that you do not have to be anybody but yourself

African American: The race group that includes people who are from the United States and have ancestors who are from the continent of Africa

ageism: Discrimination and oppression against people who are 18 and younger (children) and elders

Alaska Native: The race group that includes people who have ancestors who are indigenous to the land that is now called Alaska

American Indian: The race group that includes people who have ancestors who are indigenous to the land that is now called the United States

amplify: To make something louder

ancestors: Your family members who were born before you, including your grandparents, their grandparents, and so on

antiracism: The act of making a choice to be active and resist racism

antiracist: Making a choice to be active and resist racism

Asian: The race group that includes people who have ancestors who are from the continent of Asia

Asian American: The race group that includes people who are from the United States and have ancestors who are from the continent of Asia

bias: A belief about a person, a group of people, a place, or a thing. Usually, your biases are hidden. You are not always aware of what biases you have.

biracial: Having two different racial identities

Black: The race group that includes people who have ancestors who are from the continent of Africa

boundary: A rule or a limit that you set for yourself

boycott: When you will no longer buy things from someone or some organization because you do not agree with their words or actions

cisgender person (or cis person): A person who understands their gender to be the same as the gender the doctor said they were when they were born

cissexism: Discrimination and oppression against people who are transgender or nonbinary, or people whose gender expression does not follow the common expectations of their gender

citizen: A person who is allowed by law to be a member of a country

citizenship: Having membership in a country by law

citizenship identity: The parts of your identity that come from the countries where you are allowed by law to be a member

class: A group of people who have a similar amount of money and resources. (This is different from your classroom at school!)

class identity: The parts of your identity that come from the amount of money and resources you, your family, and other members of your class have

classism: Discrimination and oppression against people who do not have a lot of money or resources

colonization: When one group takes control of another group by force. (Most of the time, the first group uses violence to take control of the second group.)

colonize: The act of one group taking control of another group by force

colonizer: A person who is part of a group that takes control of another group by force

community:

> • A group of people living together in the same place. The place can be your neighborhood or your city or town.

> • Community can also mean a group of people who share the same ideas and goals, who care about the same things.

community service: When you work to help people in your community with things they need right away

culture: The traditions and holidays you, your family, and your community celebrate together; the things you and your family believe; and the languages you speak, read, or write together

descent: Being related to your ancestors

discriminate: To treat people unfairly, unequally, and unjustly

discrimination: The unfair, unequal, and unjust treatment of people

dismantle: To take something apart, break it, and knock it down

dominant: Having power and being controlling

dominant culture: The culture that is most powerful in our country

enslaved person: A person who never has the freedom to live their life the way they want to live it. Their society says they are owned by another person, and the enslaved person is made to work for that person for free.

equal: Having the same amount

equitable: Each person getting what they need, which may be different for different people because not everyone needs the same things

equity: When each person gets what they need, which may be different for different people because not everyone needs the same things

ethnic identity: The parts of your identity that come from the culture that your ancestors shared with you and your family

ethnicity: The parts of your identity that come from all of the people in your family who were born before you

Europeans: People from the continent of Europe

fair: Everyone getting what they need. Making sure things are equal and just for all people.

fairness: When everyone gets what they need and things are equal and just for all people

gender: The way that many people in society believe that a person should behave based on whether they have male or female body parts. A lot of people think there are just two genders, female and male, but there are many, many more!

gender identity: The parts of your identity that come from the way you understand your gender and how that understanding is similar to or different from the gender the doctor said you were when you were born

genes: Parts of your body that help to build your body, tell your body what to do, and keep you healthy. They also decide what you will look like.

genetic makeup: The genes that are passed down to you from your birth parents, their parents, and your ancestors

heterosexism: Discrimination and oppression against people based on who they love

Hispanic: The ethnic group that includes people who are from countries where Spanish is the language that most people speak

identity: Who you are! Everything that makes you *you*, from what you look like to what you think and believe to what you like to do.

identity map: Something you create that is all about who you are! You can put your social identities and your personal identities on it, and you can choose to share it with other people.

immigrant: A person who moves to a new country

indentured servant: A person who has an agreement with the person they work for to work for them for several years. After the servant works that time, they have the freedom to live their life the way they want to live it.

indigenous: The very first to live on the land and in a particular place

indigenous people: The very first people to live on the land and in a particular place. Sometimes, depending on where you live, indigenous people are called First Nations people, Native Americans, or Aboriginal people.

injustice: When not everyone gets what they need to be healthy, cared for, and safe. When some people are treated as if they are not as important as others. When people are not treated fairly.

institution: An organized group of people or several different organized groups of people working together

intersectionality: The idea that anyone can have more than just one identity at any one time and that some parts of a person's identity may give them power

just: Having everyone get what they need to be healthy, cared for, and safe. (Remember: Not everyone needs the same things to feel safe and cared for, because we are all different!)

justice: When everyone gets what they need to be healthy, cared for, and safe. (Remember: Not everyone needs the same things to feel safe and cared for, because we are all different!)

Latino/a/x/e: The ethnic group that includes people who are born in or have ancestors from Latin American countries

LGBTQQIP2AA+: People who are lesbian, gay, bisexual, transgender, questioning, queer, intersex, pansexual, two-spirit, androgynous, asexual, and more

melanin: The natural coloring of your skin. It helps to protect your skin from the sun.

microaggressions: Negative words and/or negative actions from people who are members of the dominant culture toward people who are not part of the dominant culture

minorities: A word some people use to refer to Indigenous, Black and African, Asian, and Latino/a/x/e people, even though the number of Indigenous, Black, Asian, and Latino/a/x/e people in the world is really big. (See **Person of the Global Majority** for a more positive way to talk about people!)

minority: Less than half, or a few

multiethnic: Having many ethnic identities

Native Hawaiian: The race group that includes people who have ancestors who are indigenous to Hawaii

neurological: About nerves or the nervous system

nonbinary: Does not identify only as either male or female

non-native English speaker: A person whose first language is not English

oppression: When one group of people believe they are better than another and abuse and misuse their power against the second group

organize: The act of putting things into different groups

Pacific Islander: The race group that includes people who have ancestors who are indigenous to Hawaii, Samoa, Guam, and islands located in the Pacific Ocean

Person of the Global Majority: An Indigenous, Black or African, Asian, or Latino/a/x/e person

personal identity: The parts of your identity that come from you, your family, your community, the experiences you have, and the places around you—and that make you different from other people!

power: Having control over yourself and the freedom to make choices and change

prejudice: A belief, attitude, or feeling about a person or group of people that comes from not having all of the right information. Usually, you and other people are aware of your prejudices.

pronouns: Words—like he, she, they, them, I, and my—that help to shorten sentences, so you do not need to repeat names. Pronouns are an important part of our identities.

race: What other people see when they look at a person's skin color and skin tone, hair texture, and other parts of the way they look

racial identity: The parts of your identity that come from the race (or races) that you are a part of

racial group: A group of people who share the same racial identity

racism: Personal prejudice and bias and the planned misuse and abuse of power by institutions. It is discrimination and oppression against people based on the color of their skin, their hair texture, facial features, and where their ancestors came from.

repair: To work to make things better

resist: To not give in and to stand up, sit tall, speak out, and use your power against someone or something

sexism: Discrimination and oppression against people who are not cis male

slavery: When a person or group of people forces another person or group of people to do hard work for the first person or group without pay

social construction: An idea created by people in society

social identity: The parts of your identity that relate to other people in your community and around the world. Some social identity categories are race, ethnicity, gender, citizenship, and class.

social ranking: A way to put people into different groups with some people in the top group and some people in the bottom group. People at the top of the social ranking are believed to be more important than the people who were put into the bottom.

society:

- A group of people living together in a community
- People in the larger world community

stereotype: A general idea or belief about a group of people that is not based on facts

transgender person: A person who understands their gender to be different from the gender the doctor said they were when they were born

trust: To believe that a person is telling you the truth and will do what they say they will do

United States citizen: A person who is born in the United States and is allowed by law to be a member of the country

unfair: Everyone not getting what they need

unjust: Not having everyone get what they need to be healthy, cared for, and safe. (Remember: Not everyone needs the same things to feel safe and cared for, because we are all different!)

white: The race group that includes people who have ancestors from Europe, Asia, and Africa

Books To Read To Keep Learning and Growing

The ABCs of the Black Panther Party by S. Khalilah Brann, Chemay Morales-James, and Uela May

The Ana & Andrew series, by Christine Platt, Sharon Sordo, Junissa Bianda, and Anuki López

Call and Response: The Story of Black Lives Matter by Veronica Chambers of the New York Times

Dreamers by Yuyi Morales

El's Mirror by Ellison Blakes, Bavu Blakes, and A. H. Taylor

Eyes That Kiss in the Corners by Joanna Ho and Dung Ho

"Fall in Line, Holden!" by Daniel W. Vandever

Finish the Fight!: The Brave and Revolutionary Women Who Fought for the Right to Vote by Veronica Chambers and the Staff of the New York Times

I Am Enough by Grace Byers and Keturah A. Bobo

I Am Every Good Thing by Derrick Barnes and Gordon C. James

It Feels Good to Be Yourself: A Book About Gender Identity by Theresa Thorn and Noah Grigni

a kids book about white privilege by Ben Sand

a kids book about systemic racism by Jordan Thierry

Not My Idea: A Book About Whiteness by Anastasia Higginbotham

Our Skin: A First Conversation About Race by Megan Madison, Jessica Ralli, and Isabel Roxas

The Power Book: What Is It, Who Has It, and Why? by Claire Saunders, Hazel Songhurst, Georgia Amson-Bradshaw, Minna Salami, Mik Scarlet, Joelle Avelino, and David Broadbent

Skin Again by bell hooks and Chris Raschka

Sometimes I Feel Like a Fox by Danielle Daniel

Stamped (For Kids): Racism, Antiracism, and You by Sonja Cherry-Paul, Jason Reynolds, Ibram X. Kendi, and Rachelle Baker

The Talk: Conversations about Race, Love, and Truth edited by Wade Hudson and Cheryl Willis Hudson

Tristan Strong Punches a Hole in the Sky by Kwame Mbalia

The Undefeated by Kwame Alexander and Kadir Nelson

Ways to Make Sunshine by Renée Watson and Nina Mata

What the Road Said by Cleo Wade and Lucie de Moyencourt

What We Believe: A Black Lives Matter Principles Activity Book by Laleña Garcia and Caryn Davidson

When Aidan Became a Brother by Kyle Lukoff and Kaylani Juanita

Where Are You From? by Yamile Saied Méndez and Jaime Kim

The Year of the Dog by Grace Lin

Young Native Activist: Growing Up in Native American Rights Movements by Aslan Tudor

Books for the Adult Readers
(So They Can Keep Learning and Growing Too!)

An African American and Latinx History of the United States by Paul Ortiz

Anti-Bias Education for Young Children and Ourselves by Louise Derman-Sparks and Julie Olsen Edwards

Are Prisons Obsolete? by Angela Y. Davis

A Different Mirror: A History of Multicultural America by Ronald Takaki

Ghosts in the Schoolyard by Eve L. Ewing

How the World Is Passed by Clint Smith

How We Fight White Supremacy: A Field Guide to Black Resistance by Akiba Solomon and Kenrya Rankin

An Indigenous Peoples' History of the United States for Young People by Roxanne Dunbar-Ortiz, Jean Mendoza, and Debbie Reese

Me and White Supremacy: Combat Racism, Change the World, and Become a Good Ancestor by Layla Saad

Parenting for Liberation: A Guide for Raising Black Children by Trina Greene Brown

Pushout by Monique W. Morris

So You Want to Talk About Race by Ijeoma Oluo

Stamped: Racism, Antiracism, and You (A Remix of the National Book Award–winning Stamped from the Beginning) by Jason Reynolds and Ibram X. Kendi

Start Here, Start Now: A Guide to Antibias and Antiracist Work in Your School Community by Liz Kleinrock

Teaching Community: A Pedagogy of Hope by bell hooks

Teaching/Learning Anti-Racism: A Developmental Approach by Louise Derman Sparks and Carol Brunson Phillips

Textured Teaching: A Framework for Culturally Sustaining Practices by Lorena Escota Germán

The Three Mothers: How the Mothers of Martin Luther King, Jr., Malcolm X, and James Baldwin Shaped a Nation by Anna Malaika Tubbs

This Book Is Anti-Racist: 20 Lessons on How to Wake Up, Take Action, and Do the Work by Tiffany Jewell and Aurélia Durand

This Book Is Anti-Racist Journal: Over 50 Activities to Help You Wake Up, Take Action, and Do the Work by Tiffany Jewell and Aurélia Durand

We Live for the We: The Political Power of Black Motherhood by Dani McClain

We Want to Do More Than Survive: Abolitionist Teaching and the Pursuit of Educational Freedom by Bettina Love

Why Are All the Black Kids Sitting Together in the Cafeteria? And Other Conversations About Race by Dr. Beverly Daniel Tatum

Why I'm No Longer Talking to White People About Race by Reni Eddo-Lodge